Slavoj Žižek is a Slovene philosopher and cultural critic. He is a senior researcher at the Institute for Sociology and Philosophy, University of Ljubljana, international director of the Birkbeck Institute for the Humanities and a professor of philosophy and psychoanalysis at the European Graduate School. He writes widely on a diverse range of topics, including political theory, film theory, cultural studies, theology and psychoanalysis. His books include *Living in the End Times*, *First as Tragedy, Then as Farce*, *In Defense of Lost Causes*, four volumes of the *Essential Žižek*, and many more.

Srećko Horvat is a Croatian author, philosopher and translator. He is one of the founders of the Subversive Festival, an annual conference and activist meeting in Zagreb. His latest publication is *After the End of History. From the Arab Spring to the Occupy Movement* (Laika Verlag, Germany, 2013).

WHAT DOES EUROPE WANT?

WHAT DOES EUROPE WANT?

The Union and its Discontents

SLAVOJ ŽIŽEK

SREĆKO HORVAT

First published in 2013 by
Istros Books
London, United Kingdom
www.istrosbooks.com

Artwork & Design © Milos Miljkovich, 2013
Graphic Designer/Web Developer – miljkovicmisa@gmail.com
Typeset by Octavo-Smith Ltd

ISBN: 978-1908236166

Printed in England by
CMP (UK), Poole, Dorset
www.cmp-uk.com

This edition has been made possible through the financial support granted by the Croatian Ministry of Culture.

CONTENTS

ALEXIS TSIPRAS

FOREWORD:
THE DESTRUCTION OF GREECE
AS A MODEL FOR ALL OF EUROPE.
IS THIS THE FUTURE THAT
EUROPE DESERVES?

From the middle of the 1990s until almost the end of the first decade of the twenty-first century, Greece tended towards economic growth. The main characteristics of that growth were the very large and non-taxed profits enjoyed by the rich, along with over-indebtedness and the rising unemployment among the poor. Public money was stolen in numerous ways, and the economy was limited mainly to the consumption of imported goods from rich European countries. Rating agencies considered this model of 'cheap money, cheap labour' the model of dynamic emerging economies.

The Vicious Cycle of Depression

Everything, however, changed after the 2008 crisis. The cost of the bank losses that were created by uncontrolled speculation were transfered to national governments, which were in turn transferred to society at large. The flawed model of Greek development collapsed and the country was deprived of the opportunity to borrow, causing it to become dependent on the IMF and the European bank. And all this was accompanied by an extremely severe austerity programme.

This programme, which the Greek government adopted without proper debate, consists of two parts: 'stabilisation' and 'reform'. The conditions of the programme are presented as positive, in order to cover up the huge social destruction it has caused. In Greece, the part of the programme named 'stabilisation' leads to indirect, destructive taxation, large cuts in public spending and the destruction of the welfare state, especially in the areas of health, education and social security, as well as the privatisation of basic social goods, such as water and energy. The programme which forms part of the 'reform' deals with the simplification of redundancy procedure, the elimination of collective agreements and the creation of 'special economic zones'. This is accompanied by many other regulations designed to facilitate the investment of powerful and colonialist economic forces, without the inconvenience of, say, having to go all the way to South Sudan. These are just some of the conditions that are in the 'Memorandum', the contract that was signed by Greece with the IMF, the European Union and the European Central Bank.

These measures are naturally supposed to lead Greece out of the crisis. The strict 'stabilisation' programme should lead to budget surpluses, allowing the country to stop borrowing, while at the same time enabling it to pay off the debt. On the other hand, the 'reforms' are aimed at regaining market confidence, encouraging them to invest after witnessing the destroyed welfare state and the desperate, insecure and low-paid workers in the labour market. This would lead to new 'development'; something which does not exist anywhere except in 'holy books' and the perverted minds of global neoliberalism.

It was assumed that the programme would be very effective and fast, and that Greece would soon be 'reborn' and back on the path of growth. But three years after the signing of the 'Memorandum', the situation is becoming worse. The economy is sinking further, and the taxes are obviously not collected, for the simple reason that the Greek citizens are unable to pay them. The reduction of spending has now reached the core of social integrity, creating the conditions of a humanitarian crisis. In other words, we are now talking about people who are reduced to eating rubbish and sleeping on the pavements, about pensioners who can not afford to buy bread, of households without electricity, of patients who are unable to afford medicine and treatment. And all this within the eurozone.

Investors, of course, do not come, given that the current bankruptcy option remains open. And of course, the authors of the 'Memorandum' after each tragic failure, react by imposing more taxes and more cuts. The Greek economy has entered a vicious cycle of uncontrolled depression that leads nowhere except to complete disaster.

Taliban Neoliberalism

The Greek 'rescue' plan (another convenient term used to describe this disaster) ignores a fundamental principle. The economy is like a cow: it eats grass and produces milk. It is inconceivable to take away a quarter of her grass and expect her to produce four times more milk. The cow will simply die. The same is now happening to the Greek economy.

The Greek Left realised, from the very first moment, that the austerity measures would not 'cure', but actually deepen the crisis. When someone is drowning, he needs to be thrown a lifeline, not a weight. For their part, the Taliban neoliberalists still assure us that things will improve. Yet even the most stupid among them must now know that this is a lie. But this stance is not nonsense, and it's not dogmatism. The leaders of the IMF themselves recently stated that there is an error in the design of the Greek austerity programme, which is doomed to failure, and that the effects of the recession are completely out of control. And yet the programme continues with an unprecedented stubbornness and persistence, and the situation is becoming more and more difficult. The conclusion can only be that something else lies behind all this.

In fact, behind all this is the fact that pulling the Greek economy out of the crisis is not in the interests of Europe or the IMF. Much more important is the desire to remove, as the ultimate goal of the programme, what in post-war Europe became known as the 'social contract'. The fact that Greece will be left bankrupt and riddled with social problems is not important. What is important, is that a eurozone country is openly discussing the introduction of a wage level comparative to that of the Chinese, along with the abolition of workers' rights, the abolition of national insurance and the welfare state, and the total privatisation of utilities and public goods. Those neoliberal depraved minds, who already encountered violent resistance in European societies following the decade of the 1990s, now find their dream becoming a reality through the pretext of the crisis.

Greece is the first step. The debt crisis has already spread to other countries in southern Europe, and penetrates deeper into the heart of the European Union. Greece can serve as a case study. Anyone who is exposed to the speculative attacks of the markets has no other choice but to destroy the remnants of the welfare state, as has happened in Greece. Similar memoranda in Spain and Portugal have already introduced similar changes. But this strategy is fully revealed in the 'European Pact for Stability', which promotes Germany in place of the entire Union. Member states are no longer free to manage their own finances. The central institutions of the EU are allowed to intervene in budgets and impose tough fiscal measures to reduce deficits. This policy strongly affects schools, nurseries, universities, public hospitals and social programmes. If people use democracy as a defence against austerity, as happened recently in Italy, the result for democracy is even worse.

There Are Alternatives

Let us be clear: the generalised European model was not created in order to save Greece, but to destroy it. Europe's future is already planned and it envisages happy bankers and unhappy societies. In the anticipated development plan, capital will be the rider and society will be the horse. It's an ambitious plan, but it can not go far. The reason is that not one such project was ever completed without the consensus of society and the protection of its most vulnerable. It seems that the leading European elite has currently forgotten this fact. Unfortunately for them, they will have to face up to it sooner than they think.

It is the beginning of the end of the existing neoliberal capitalism; the most aggressive capitalism that mankind has ever faced, and which has dominated for the past two decades. Ever since the collapse of Lehman Brothers, there have been two conflicting strategies for overcoming the crisis which represent two different perspectives on the world economy. The first strategy is a financial expansion, with the printing of new money, the nationalisation of banks and the increased taxation of the rich. The other is by saving, transferring the bank debt to the public sector debt, relying on the middle and lower classes of society being overly taxed, while only the rich can avoid tax altogether. European leaders choose another model, but they too have come to a standstill, while facing additional problems. These problems led to an historic conflict in Europe. A conflict that seemingly has geographical dimensions and designations: on the surface it seems to be divided into that of north-south, yet beneath the surface there is a class conflict that relates to two conflicting strategies for Europe. One strategy defends the complete domination of capital, unconditionally and without principles, and without any plan for secure social cohesion and welfare. The other strategy defends European democracy and social needs. The conflict has already begun.

There is an alternative solution to the crisis. This is to protect European companies from the speculation of financial capital. It is the emancipation of the real economy from the constraints of profit. It is a way out of monetarism and authoritative fiscal policy. It is a new development planning with social benefits as the main criterion. It is a new production model, based on decent work conditions, the expansion of public good and environmental protection. This view is consistently left out of the discussion by the European leadership. It remains with the people, the European workers and already 'bitter' movements to strike their own stamp on history and prevent the mass looting and destruction.

The experience of previous years leads to one conclusion: there is one morality in politics and another for economy. In the years since 1989, the morality of the economy has fully prevailed over the ethics of politics and democracy. What went in favour of the two, those five or ten strong financial institutions, were considered legitimate, even if it would be contrary to fundamental human rights principles. Today our task is to restore the dominance of political and social moral values, as opposed to the logic of profit.

The War of Resistance

How will we make the dynamics of social struggle work? And how can we break, once and for all, the harness of social apathy on which the construction of Europe since 1989 is founded upon? The active participation of the masses in politics is the only thing that can frighten the ruling elite in Europe and worldwide. And that's exactly why we should make it happen.

The plan for a stronger economic cycle is clear. We need to create a different political and social project and defend it by all means at the central and local level. Let's start with the workplace, with universities and neighbourhoods, until we have a coordinated joint action in all European countries. It is a struggle of resistance that will result in a victory as long as it leads to a common alternative programme for Europe. Today's conflict is not one between deficit and surplus countries, or between disciplined and restless people. Today's conflict is between the European social interests and the needs of capital for continual profit growth.

We will defend social interests, or else our future and our children's future will be uncertain and dark, something that in recent decades we could not even imagine. The model for development that was based on the 'free market' is now bankrupt. At this time the dominant forces are attacking society, its unity and all the privileges that it has managed to retain. This is what is happening in Greece, and this is the plan for the whole of Europe. Let us therefore defend ourselves by any means. We must support a social resistance that invokes and permanently upholds a sense of solidarity and a unified strategy for the peoples of Europe.

The future does not belong to neoliberalism, bankers and a few powerful multinational companies. The future belongs to the nation and to society. It's time to open the way for a democratic, socially cohesive and free Europe. Because this is the only viable, realistic and feasible solution to exit the current crisis.

Greece
March 2013

Slavoj Žižek

I

Breaking Our Eggs Without the Omelette, from Cyprus to Greece

There is a story (apocryphal, maybe) about the Left-leaning, Keynesian economist, John Galbraith: before a trip to the USSR in the late 1950s, he wrote to his anti-communist friend Sidney Hook: 'Don't worry, I will not be seduced by the Soviets and return home claiming they have socialism!' Hook answered him promptly: 'But that's what worries me – that you will return claiming that the USSR is NOT socialist!' What worried Hook was the naive defence of the purity of the concept: if things go wrong with building a Socialist society, this does not invalidate the idea itself, it just means we didn't implement it properly.

Do we not detect the same naivety in today's market funda-mentalists? When, during a recent TV debate in France, Guy Sorman claimed that democracy and capitalism necessarily go together, I couldn't resist asking him the obvious question: 'But what about China today?' He snapped back: 'In China there is no capitalism!' For a fanatically pro-capitalist Sorman, if a country is non-democratic, it simply means it is not truly capitalist but practises its disfigured version, in exactly the same way that for a democratic communist, Stalinism was simply not an authentic form of communism.

The underlying mistake is not difficult to identify – it is the same as in the well-known joke: 'My fiancée is never late for an appointment; because the moment she is late she is no longer my fiancée!' This is how today's apologist of the market, in an unheard-of ideological kidnapping, explains the crisis of 2008: it was not the failure of the free market which caused it but the excessive state regulation, i.e. the fact that our market economy was not a true one, that it was still in the clutches of the welfare state. When we stick to such a purity of market capitalism, dismissing its failures as accidental mishaps, we end up in a naive progressivism whose exemplary case is the Christmas issue of *The Spectator* magazine (15 December 2012). It opens up with the editorial 'Why 2012 was the best year ever', which argues against the perception that we live in 'a dangerous, cruel world where things are bad and getting worse'. Here is the opening paragraph:

> It may not feel like it, but 2012 has been the greatest year in the history of the world. That sounds like an extravagant claim, but it is borne out by evidence. Never has there been less hunger, less disease or more prosperity. The West remains in the economic doldrums, but most developing countries are charging ahead, and people are being lifted out of poverty at the fastest rate ever recorded. The death toll inflicted by war and natural disasters is also mercifully low. We are living in a golden age.[1]

The same idea was developed in detail by Matt Ridley. Here is the blurb for his *The Rational Optimist*:

> A counterblast to the prevailing pessimism of our age, and proves, however much we like to think to the contrary, that

things are getting better. Over 10,000 years ago there were fewer than 10 million people on the planet. Today there are more than 6 billion, 99 per cent of whom are better fed, better sheltered, better entertained and better protected against disease than their Stone Age ancestors. The availability of almost everything a person could want or need has been going erratically upwards for 10,000 years and has rapidly accelerated over the last 200 years: calories; vitamins; clean water; machines; privacy; the means to travel faster than we can run, and the ability to communicate over longer distances than we can shout. Yet, bizarrely, however much things improve from the way they were before, people still cling to the belief that the future will be nothing but disastrous.[2]

And there is more of the same. Here is the blurb for Steven Pinker's *The Better Angels of Our Nature*:

Believe it or not, today we may be living in the most peaceful moment in our species' existence. In his gripping and controversial new work, New York Times bestselling author Steven Pinker shows that despite the ceaseless news about war, crime, and terrorism, violence has actually been in decline over long stretches of history. Exploding myths about humankind's inherent violence and the curse of modernity, this ambitious book continues Pinker's exploration of the essence of human nature, mixing psychology and history to provide a remarkable picture of an increasingly enlightened world.[3]

With many provisos, one can roughly accept the data to which these 'rationalists' refer – yes, today we definitely live better than our ancestors did 10,000 years ago in the Stone Age, and even an average prisoner in Dachau (the Nazi working camp, not in Auschwitz, the killing camp) was living at least marginally better than, probably, a slave prisoner of the Mongols. Etc. etc. – but there is something that this story misses.

There is a more down-to-earth version of the same insight which one often hears in mass media, in the quoted passage from *The Spectator* but especially those of non-European countries: crisis? What crisis? Look at the BRIC countries, at Poland, South Korea, Singapore, Peru, even many sub-Saharan African states – they are all progressing. The losers are only Western Europe and, up to a point, the US, so we are not dealing with a global crisis, but just with the shift of the dynamics of progress away from the West. Is a portent symbol of this shift not the fact that, recently, many people from Portugal, a country in deep crisis, are returning to Mozambique and Angola, ex-colonies of Portugal, but this time as economic immigrants, not as colonisers? So what if our much-decried crisis is a mere local crisis in an overall progress? Even with regard to human rights: is the situation in China and Russia now not better than fifty years ago? Decrying the ongoing crisis as a global phenomenon is thus a typical Eurocentrist view, and a view coming from Leftists who usually pride themselves on their anti-Eurocentrism.

But we should restrain our anti-colonialist joy here – the question to be raised is: if Europe is in gradual decay, what is replacing its hegemony? The answer is: 'capitalism with Asian values' – which, of course, has nothing to do with Asian people and everything to do with the clear and present tendency of contemporary capitalism, as such, to suspend democracy. From Marx on, the truly radical Left was never simply 'progressivist' – it was always obsessed by the question: what is the price of progress? Marx was fascinated by capitalism, by the unheard-of productivity it unleashed; he just insisted that this very success engenders antagonisms. And we should do the same with today's progress of global capitalism: keep in view its dark underside which is fomenting revolts.

People rebel not when 'things are really bad', but when their expectations are disappointed. The French Revolution occurred after the king and the nobles were for decades gradually losing their full hold on power; the 1956 anti-communist revolt in Hungary exploded after Nagy Imre had already been prime minister for two years, after (relatively) free debates among intellectuals; people rebelled in Egypt in 2011 because there was some economic progress under Mubarak, giving rise to a whole class of educated young people who participated in the universal digital culture. And this is why the Chinese communists are right to panic, precisely because, on average, the Chinese are now living considerably better than forty years ago – but the social antagonisms (between the newly rich and the rest) exploded, plus expectations are much higher. That's the problem with development and progress: they are always uneven, they give birth to new instabilities and antagonisms, and they generate new expectations which cannot be met. In Tunisia or Egypt just prior to the Arab Spring, the majority probably lived a little bit better than decades ago, but the standards by which they measured their (dis)satisfaction were much higher.

So yes, *The Spectator*, Ridley, Pinker etc. are in principle right, but the very facts that they emphasise are creating conditions for revolt and rebellion. Recall the classic cartoon scene of a cat who simply continues to walk over the edge of the precipice, ignoring that she no longer has ground under her feet – she falls down only when she looks down and notices she is hanging in the abyss. Is this not how ordinary people in Cyprus must feel these days? They are aware that Cyprus will never be the same, that there is a catastrophic fall in the standard of living ahead, but the full impact of this fall is not yet properly felt, so for a short period they can afford to go on with their normal daily lives like the cat who calmly walks in the empty air. And we should not condemn them: such delaying of the full crash is also a surviving strategy – the real impact will come silently when the panic will be over. This is why it is now, when the Cyprus crisis has largely disappeared from the media, that one should think and write about it.

There is a well-known joke from the last decade of the Soviet Union about Rabinovitch, a Jew who wants to emigrate. The bureaucrat at the emigration office asks him why, and Rabinovitch answers: 'There are two reasons why. The first is that I'm afraid that in the Soviet Union the communists will lose power, and the new power will put all the blame for the communist crimes on us Jews – there will again be anti-Jewish pogroms ...' The bureaucrat interrupts him: 'But this is pure nonsense. Nothing can change in the Soviet Union; the power of the communists will last forever!' Rabinovitch responds calmly: 'Well, that's my second reason.'

It is easy to imagine a similar conversation between a European Union financial administrator and a Cypriote Rabinovitch today – Rabinovitch complains: 'There are two reasons we are in a panic here. First, we are afraid that the EU will simply abandon Cyprus and let our economy collapse ...' The EU administrator interrupts him: 'But you can trust us, we will not abandon you, we will tightly control you and advise you what to do!' Rabinovitch responds calmly: 'Well, that's my second reason.'

Such a deadlock effectively renders the core of the sad predicament of Cyprus: it cannot survive in prosperity without Europe, but also not with Europe – both options are worse, as Stalin would have put it. Recall the cruel joke from Lubitsch's film *To Be or Not to Be*: when asked about the German concentration camps in occupied Poland, responsible Nazi officer 'Concentration Camp Ehrhardt' snaps back: 'We do the concentrating, and the Poles do the camping.' Does the same not hold for the ongoing financial crisis in Europe? The strong Northern Europe, focused in Germany, does the concentrating, while the weakened and vulnerable South does the camping. What is emerging on the horizon are thus the contours of a divided Europe: its Southern part will be more and more reduced to a zone with a cheaper labour force, outside the safety network of the welfare state, a domain appropriate for outsourcing and tourism. In short, the gap between the developed world and those lagging behind will now run within Europe itself.

This gap is reflected in the two main stories about Cyprus which resemble the two earlier stories about Greece. There is what can be called the German story: free spending, debts and money laundering cannot go on indefinitely, etc. And there is the Cyprus story: the brutal EU measures amount to a new German occupation which is depriving Cyprus of its sovereignty. Both stories are wrong, and the demands they imply are nonsensical: Cyprus by definition cannot repay its debt, while Germany and the EU cannot simply go on throwing money to fill in the Cypriot financial hole. Both stories obfuscate the key fact: that there is something wrong with the entire system in which uncontrollable banking speculations can cause a whole country to go bankrupt. The Cyprus crisis is not a storm in the cup of a small marginal country; it is a symptom of what is wrong with the entire EU system.

This is why the solution is not just more regulation to prevent money laundering etc., but (at least) a radical change in the entire banking system – to say the unsayable, some kind of socialisation of banks. The lesson to be taken from the crashes that accumulated worldwide from 2008 on (Wall Street,

Iceland ...) is clear: the whole network of financial funds and transactions, from individual deposits and retirement funds up to the functioning of all kinds of derivatives, will have to be somehow put under social control, streamlined and regulated. This may sound utopian, but the true utopia is the notion that we can somehow survive with small cosmetic changes.

But there is a fatal trap to be avoided here: the socialisation of banks that is needed is not a compromise between wage labour and productive capital against the power of finance. Financial meltdowns and crises are obvious reminders that the circulation of capital is not a closed loop which can fully sustain itself, i.e., that this circulation points towards the reality of producing and selling actual goods that satisfy actual people's needs. However, the more subtle lesson of crises and meltdowns is that there is no return to this reality – all the rhetoric of 'let us move from the virtual space of financial speculations back to real people who produce and consume' is deeply misleading; it is ideology at its purest. The paradox of capitalism is that you cannot throw out the dirty water of financial speculations and keep the healthy baby of real economy: the dirty water effectively is the 'bloodline' of the healthy baby.

What this simply means is that the solution of the Cyprus crisis does not reside in Cyprus. For Cyprus to get a chance, something will have to change elsewhere. Otherwise we will all remain caught in the madness that distorts our behaviour in times of crises. Here is how Marx defines the traditional miser as 'a capitalist gone mad', hoarding his treasure in a secret hideout, in contrast to the 'normal' capitalist who augments his treasure by throwing it into circulation[4]:

The restless never-ending process of profit-making alone is what he aims at. This boundless greed after riches, this passionate chase after exchange-value, is common to the capitalist and the miser; but while the miser is merely a capitalist gone mad, the capitalist is a rational miser. The never-ending augmentation of exchange-value, which the miser strives after, by seeking to save his money from circulation, is attained by the more acute capitalist, by constantly throwing it afresh into circulation.

This madness of the miser is nonetheless not something which simply disappears with the rise of 'normal' capitalism, or its pathological deviation. It is rather inherent to it: the miser has his moment of triumph in the economic crisis. In a crisis, it is not – as one would expect – money which loses its value, and we have to resort to the 'real' value of commodities; commodities themselves (the embodiment of 'real /use/ value') become useless, because there is no-one to buy them. In a crisis, 'money suddenly and immediately changes from its merely nominal shape, money of account, into hard cash. Profane commodities can no longer replace it. The use-value of commodities becomes value-less, and their value vanishes in the face of their own form of value. The bourgeois, drunk with prosperity and arrogantly certain of itself, has just declared that money is a purely imaginary creation. 'Commodities alone are money,' it said. But now the opposite cry resounds over the markets of the world: only money is a commodity ... 'In a crisis, the antithesis between commodities and their value-form, money, is raised to the level of an absolute contradiction.'[5]

Does this not mean that at this moment, far from disintegrating, fetishism is fully asserted in its direct madness? In crisis, the underlying belief, disavowed and just practised, is thus directly asserted. And the same holds for today's ongoing crisis: one of the spontaneous reactions to it is to turn to some commonsense guideline: 'Debts have to be paid!', 'You cannot spend more than you produced!', or something similar – and this, of course, is the worst thing one can do, since in this way, one gets caught in a downward spiral. First, such elementary wisdom is simply wrong – the United States was doing quite well for decades spending much more than it produced.

At a more fundamental level, we should clearly perceive the paradox of debt: at the direct material level of social totality, debts are in a way irrelevant, inexistent even, since humanity as a whole consumes what it produces – by definition, one cannot consume more. One can reasonably speak of debt only with regard to natural resources (destroying the material conditions for the survival of future generations), where we are indebted to future generations which, precisely, do not yet exist and which, not without irony, will come to exist only through – and thus be indebted for their existence to – ourselves. So here also, the term 'debt' has no literal sense, it cannot be 'financialised', quantified into an amount of money. The debt we can talk about occurs when, within a global society, some group (nation or whichever) consumes more than it produces, which means that another group has to consume less than it produces – but here, relations are not as simple and clear as it may appear. Relations would be clear if, in a situation of debt, money would just have been a neutral instrument measuring how much more one group consumed with regard to what it produced, and at whose expense – but the actual situation is far from this. According to public data, around 90 per cent of money circulating around is the virtual credit money; so if 'real' producers find themselves indebted to financial institutions, one has good reason to doubt the status of their debt – how much of it was the result of speculations which happened in a sphere without any link to the reality of a local unit of production?

So when a country finds itself under the pressure of

international financial institutions, be it IMF or private banks, one should always bear in mind that their pressure (translated into concrete demands: reduce public spending by dismantling parts of the welfare state, privatise, open up your market, deregulate your banks ...) is not the expression of some neutral objective, logic or knowledge, but of a doubly partial ('interested') knowledge: at the formal level, it is a knowledge which embodies a series of neoliberal presuppositions, while at the level of content, it privileges the interests of certain states or institutions (banks etc.).

When the Turkish communist writer Panait Istrati visited the Soviet Union in the mid-1930s, the time of the big purges and show trials, a Soviet apologist trying to convince him about the need of violence against the enemies evoked the proverb, 'You can't make an omelette without breaking eggs', to which Istrati tersely replied, 'All right. I can see the broken eggs. Where's this omelette of yours?' But we should say the same about the austerity measures imposed by the IMF: the Greeks would have the full right to say, 'OK, we are breaking our eggs for all of Europe, but where's the omelette you are promising us?'

SREĆKO HORVAT

2

DANKE DEUTSCHLAND!

Danke Deutschland, meine Seele brennt!
Danke Deutschland, für das liebe Geschenk.
Danke Deutschland, vielen Dank,
wir sind jetzt nicht allein,
und die Hoffnung kommt in das zerstörte Heim.[6]

Croatian song, 1992

At the end of 2012, the German President Joachim Gauck visited Croatia. For some reason, I had the honour to be one of three Croatian intellectuals chosen to meet him and have a closed-room conversation about Croatia's entry to the European Union, but mainly focused on the intellectual and cultural sphere.

When you are invited to meet a president, if you are not a complete idiot, the immediate reaction should be the famous Lacanian lesson that 'a madman who believes he is king is no madder than a king who believes he is king.' In other words, a king who believes he possesses an inherent 'king gene' is implicitly mad. And the same goes for presidents. A 'president' is a symbolical function, even if – or, especially if – he is from Germany (where Angela Merkel runs the game).

In the end, I was pleasantly surprised. It was really interesting to chat with Mr Gauck. He wasn't just kindly present waiting for the official programme to end, but posed many different questions and showed interest in the Balkans. Although it was planned that culture had to be the main topic of our conversation, politics was in the air. Knowing him not only as an '*unverbesserlicher Antikommunist*' ('incorrigible anti-communist', as the Stasi described Gauck in their file on him), but also as a former Lutheran pastor and someone who seriously studied theology, at one point I asked him a question about the relation between theology and debt, with a political subtext, of course. The question was based on a manuscript from the thirteenth century cited by Jacques Le Goff:

> Usurers sin against nature by wanting to make money give birth to money, as a horse gives birth to a horse, or a mule to a mule. Usurers are in addition thieves, for they sell time that does not belong to them, and selling someone else's property, despite its owner, is theft. In addition, since they sell nothing other than the expectation of money, that is to say, time, they sell days and nights.[7]

Le Goff offers a detailed analysis of how between the twelfth and fifteenth century a caste of tradesmen developed from a small and despised group into a powerful force not only influencing social relations or even architecture, but first and foremost – social time. What is, according to Le Goff, the hypothesis of the trading activity? Exact timing: the accumulation of supplies in anticipation of famine – buying and selling at optimum moments. In other words, what Le Goff wants to show is that – before the emergence of usurers – in the Middle Ages, time still belonged to God (or to the

Church), but today it is primarily the object of capitalist expropriation/appropriation.[8]

Gauck's answer about the function of debt was this: 'It is a matter of responsibility.' Unfortunately, at this precise moment, as much as I was tempted to do so, I was polite enough not to graze the symbolic function of the President anymore. The question I wanted to pose was, of course, the following one: 'Is it the responsibility of the German bankers, or of the Greek citizens who depend on the credit?'

And it is not only a question about capitalist domination or financial speculation; it is a theological question *par excellence*. If our future is sold, then there is no future at all.

And here we come to an interesting episode from recent Croatian history. When at the end of 2012 General Ante Goto-vina, considered by many in Croatia as a war hero but ten years ago the biggest obstacle to the European *future* of Croatia, was freed from the International Court of Justice in The Hague after seven years of imprisonment, the first thing he did when he arrived back was give a speech at the central square in the capital of Croatia, where he offered a calm and terse message to the gathered crowd of 100,000 people: 'The war belongs to the past; let's turn to the future!' Among primarily emotional and some nationalist reverberations, this was the most sober message. But only at first sight.

Only a few days later, asked by a Serbian journalist about his stance towards the return of exiled Serbs to territories liberated by the operation 'Storm' ('Oluja'), the General answered: 'This is still their home, and I don't have to invite them back, since you can't invite someone to his own home.' He concluded with: 'But let's turn to the future!' The motive of the future as the main motto of the freed general was best summarised by his lawyer during a Croatian TV show. Asked what the General, now the single most popular person in

Croatia, would do with his popularity, the lawyer answered succinctly: 'He will use his popularity to promote the future.' He added that the acquittal didn't only justify the past, but also saved the future. Of course, what he forgot to add was that his future was business. Recently he invested in the gasification in his hometown Zadar, worth almost 800,000 euro. So finally, after the war and all this international justice business, we can take what we were fighting for in war – democracy and a free market!

The unavoidable irony of this hyperinflation of the future lies in the fact that never since the break-up of Yugoslavia and the end of the war was there so much public debate and discussion about the past – not about the future. Not only people on the streets, but distinguished political analysts declared that only now 'the war is over' and that Croatia was finally 'free', which could only mean that until now all of us lived in the past. All of a sudden we were ejected into the future. Politicians, public intellectuals, newspapers, TV shows – all were full of confronting the past, resembling the period in Germany during the 1960s: on the one hand, what did the operation 'Storm' really mean (now the Hague Tribunal verdict had made it clear it was legitimised as a liberation operation), and on the other hand, what crimes were still inflicted on the Serbian minority (since the generals were freed, who was now responsible for the crimes that *did* happen?). Instead of falling into this trap of what Hegel would call 'die schlechte Unendlichkeit' (once again all the endless debates were about who killed more people and whose actions and victims were more justified), the General focused himself on the future.

But what does the future really look like? As happens in rare moments, history was condensed within just a few days: at the end of 2012 the Croatian public was surprised by two other judgments that are not only giving a new meaning to the past, but also determining the future. The first verdict was against the former minister of economy, Radomir Čačić, who caused a traffic accident with two fatalities in Hungary in 2010. Although the minister was fully aware that there was a high chance he would end up in jail, he was behaving as if this didn't concern him as the most important Croatian politician at that time. In a way, the fate of the country was held hostage by his past – because it was clear that he would be convicted, there was no future in his decisions or in his (austerity and privatisation) strategy. The second verdict was a ten-year prison sentence for the former prime minister for 'war profiteering'. Among other things, Ivo Sanader was found guilty because between 1994 and 1995, during the war, he conferred high-interest rates on loans for Croatia, taking a commission of 5 per cent, which was around 7 million shillings. In other words, what he did during the 1990s directly affected the future of Croatia – namely today's external debt.

As we can see, the future didn't die during those seven years when General Gotovina was in prison. The death of the future is inscribed in the very nation-building process. Yes, Croats fought in the war, and many fought really defending their homes and families, truly believing in a better Croatia. But at the same time, the ones who convinced them to fight for Croatia worked hard to steal the future. Sanader setting high-interest rates is the best example. And the other is the once state-owned oil company INA, which is now Hungarian. And there are a number of other cases, which date back to telecommunications, another once-profitable industry that is now German, while all the doors are now open to privatisation of the railway, energy sector, healthcare system etc.

And here again we return to Gotovina and his 'promotion of the future'. If you think that his vision of the future is an empty gesture without any content, think again. What did the

General do right before the Croatians voted in the referendum on joining the EU? Although during his time in prison he hesitated to give any political messages, just a day before the EU referendum he urged all Croatian citizens to go to the referendum and vote for the European Union – and, to be sure the future would be certain, he himself voted in The Hague's prison cell. It is precisely this perspective which can give us a clear explanation of this hyperinflation of the future, which now gets a clear outline. Just a few days after his 'futuristic speech' in Zagreb, he visited the coastal city of Zadar where he admitted that his vision of future was the European Union. Then, eventually, he released a dove of peace into the air.

But doesn't the future seem a bit different? A long time ago, on one of Zagreb's façades stood a famous graffiti: 'We don't have Cash, how about MasterCard?' (Namely, the translation of 'Gotovina' is neither more nor less than 'Cash'.) Today we have both, General Gotovina and MasterCard, but we don't have any cash – we live in an economy of debt. Here the insights of the Italian philosopher Franco 'Bifo' Berardi, known for his thesis about semio-capitalism as the new form of capitalism (financialisation as a process of sign-making), could be useful. In his book *The Uprising: On Poetry and Finance*, he claims that banking is actually about storing time. In a sense, in banks we are storing our past, but also our future. Bifo goes a step further and claims that German banks are full of our time: 'The German banks have stored Greek time, Portuguese time, Italian time, and Irish time, and now the German banks are asking for their money back. They have stored the futures of the Greeks, the Portuguese, the Italians, and so on. Debt is actually future time – a promise about the future.'[9]

And if we now interpret the conversation with President Gauck, aren't precisely German or Austrian banks, among others, storing Croatian time as well? Most of the citizens – not only in Croatia, but in the whole region of the Balkans – are now highly indebted, owing money to foreign-owned banks that have spread around the Balkans and control its whole financial sector. According to some estimation, 75.3 per cent of banks in Serbia, 90 per cent in Croatia and up to 95 per cent in Bosnia and Herzegovina actually belong to German, Italian and French banks.[10] The integration of the Balkans into the EU already started twenty years ago!

So, what we should do today is to repeat the famous slogan 'Danke Deutschland', but of course, in a cynical manner. When Germany recognised Croatia as an independent state in December 1991, a Croatian singer performed a song under the title 'Danke Deutschland' on national television. Although the kitschy song actually wasn't very popular in Croatia, it clearly shows the prevailing atmosphere: this was the time when many villages and towns in Croatia had a Genscher Street or a Genscher Square, named after the German foreign minister, and even today there are some cafés having his name. As was expected, the song 'Danke Deutschland' was immediately used – and played rather more often – in Serbia as a mean of counterpropaganda, which claimed this was further proof of the eternal relationship between Germany and Croatia, namely between the 'Third Reich' and the Ustaša regime in Croatia. TV Belgrade went even so far as to play the clip for 'Danke Deutschland' over filmed scenes of crowds greeting Germans in the middle of Zagreb at the beginning of the Second World War. Why is it so impossible to imagine such an enthusiasm regarding the enlargement of today's Europe?

In an early text published during the war, in 1992, Slavoj Žižek developed the famous thesis that the Balkan 'ethnic dance macabre' was actually a symptom of Europe, reminding us of a story about an anthropological expedition trying to contact in New Zealand a tribe which allegedly danced a terrible war dance in grotesque death masks. When the members of the expedition reached the tribe, they asked the village to perform it for them, and next morning the performed dance did in fact match the description. The expedition was very satisfied; they returned to civilisation and published a much-praised report on the savage rites of the primitives. But here comes the surprise: shortly afterwards, another expedition arrived at this tribe and they found out that this terrible dance actually didn't exist in itself at all. It was created by the aborigines who somehow guessed what the strangers wanted and quickly invented it for them, to satisfy their demand. In other words, the explorers received back from the aborigines their own message. And, as you can guess, Žižek's point is that people like Hans-Dietrich Genscher were the 1990s version of the New Zealand expedition: 'They act and react in the same way, overlooking how the spectacle of old hatreds erupting in their primordial cruelty is a dance staged for their eyes, a dance for which the West is thoroughly responsible. The fantasy which organised the perception of ex-Yugoslavia is that of the Balkans as the Other of the West: the place of savage ethnic conflicts long ago overcome by civilised Europe, the place where nothing is forgotten and nothing learned, where old traumas are being replayed again and again, where symbolic links are simultaneously devalued (dozens of cease-fires broken) and overvalued (the primitive warrior's notions of honour and pride).'[11] But far from being the Other of Europe, ex-Yugoslavia was rather Europe itself in its Otherness, the screen onto which Europe projected its own repressed reverse.

And doesn't the same hold for the peripheral countries of Europe as well? Isn't Greece, soon joined by Croatia, today's mirror of Europe and all what is repressed in the centre? On the one hand, considering the Balkans still as 'the Other of the West', just before the entrance of Croatia to the EU, the European Commission engaged a London-based public relations agency – which usually worked for Coca-Cola, JP Morgan Chase and British Airways – at a cost of 20 million euro to 'break the myths and misconceptions about EU enlargement' and to ensure Croatia's accession was smooth.[12] On the other hand, like the aborigines of New Zealand, trying to fit into the Western fantasy, Croatia's government had to spend 600,000 euro, just before the referendum on the EU, to convince the Croats they would soon become part of civilised Europe.

Already these two details show that the enlargement of the EU is definitely not what it has been before. There is no optimism in the air anymore. And the true question still remains: what does Europe want? And whose responsibility is it for the current state of Europe? This is something this book will try to show, not only questioning the responsibility of the European elites but also rethinking the responsibility of the Left.

Slavoj Žižek

3

WHEN THE BLIND ARE LEADING THE BLIND, DEMOCRACY IS THE VICTIM

In one of the last interviews before his fall, Nicolae Ceausescu was asked by a western journalist how he justified the fact that Romanian citizens could not travel freely abroad although freedom of movement was guaranteed by the constitution. His answer was in the best tradition of Stalinist sophistry: true, the constitution guarantees freedom of movement, but it also guarantees the right to a safe, prosperous home. So we have here a potential conflict of rights: if Romanian citizens were to be allowed to leave the country, the prosperity of their homeland would be threatened. In this conflict, one has to make a choice, and the right to a prosperous, safe homeland enjoys clear priority.

It seems that this same spirit is alive and well in today's Slovenia, where, on 19 December 2012, the constitutional court found that a referendum on legislation to set up a 'bad bank' and a sovereign holding would be unconstitutional – in effect banning a popular vote on the matter. The referendum was proposed by trade unions challenging the government's neo-liberal economic politics, and the proposal got enough signatures to make it obligatory.

The idea of the 'bad bank' was of a place to transfer all bad credit from main banks, which would then be salvaged by state money (i.e. at taxpayers' expense), so preventing any serious inquiry into who was responsible for this bad credit in the first place. This measure, debated for months, was far from being generally accepted, even by financial specialists. So why prohibit the referendum? In 2011, when George Papandreou's government in Greece proposed a referendum on austerity measures, there was panic in Brussels, but even there no one dared to directly prohibit it.

According to the Slovenian constitutional court, the referendum 'would have caused unconstitutional consequences'. How? The court conceded a constitutional right to a referendum, but claimed that its execution would endanger other constitutional values that should be given priority in an economic crisis: the efficient functioning of the state apparatus, especially in creating conditions for economic growth; the realisation of human rights, especially the rights to social security and to free economic initiative.

In short, in assessing the consequences of the referendum, the court simply accepted as fact that failing to obey the dictates of international financial institutions (or to meet their expectations) can lead to political and economic crisis, and is thus unconstitutional. To put it bluntly: since meeting these dictates and expectations is the condition of maintaining the constitutional order, they have priority over the constitution (and eo ipso state sovereignty).

No wonder, then, that the Court's decision shocked many legal specialists. Dr France Bučar, an old dissident and one of the fathers of Slovene independence, pointed out that, following the logic the CC used in this case, it can prohibit any referendum, since every such act has social consequences: 'With this decision, the constitutional judges issued to themselves a blank check allowing them to prohibit anything anyone can concoct. Since when does the CC have the right to assess the state of economy or bank institutions? It can assess only if a certain legal regulation is in accord with the constitution or not. That's it!' There effectively can be a conflict between different rights guaranteed by constitution: say, if a group of people proposes an openly racist referendum, asking the people to endorse a law endorsing police torture, it should undoubtedly be prohibited. However, the reason for prohibition is in this case a direct conflict of the principle promoted by the referendum with other articles of the constitution; while in the Slovene case, the reason for prohibition does not concern principles, but (possible) pragmatic consequences of an economic measure.

Slovenia may be a small country, but this decision is a symptom of a global tendency towards the limitation of democracy. The idea is that, in a complex economic situation like todays, the majority of the people are not qualified to decide – they are unaware of the catastrophic consequences that would ensue if their demands were to be met. This line of argument is not new. In a TV interview a couple of years ago, the sociologist Ralf Dahrendorf linked the growing distrust for democracy to the fact that, after every revolutionary change, the road to new prosperity leads through a 'valley of tears'. After the breakdown of socialism, one cannot directly pass to the abundance of a successful market economy: limited, but real, socialist welfare and security have to be dismantled, and these first steps are necessarily painful. The same goes for western Europe, where the passage from the post-second world war welfare state to new global economy involves painful renunciations, less security, less guaranteed social care. For Dahrendorf, the problem is encapsulated by the simple fact that this painful passage through the 'valley of tears' lasts longer than the average period between elections, so that the temptation is to postpone the difficult changes for the short-term electoral gains.

For him, the paradigm here is the disappointment of the large strata of post-communist nations with the economic results of the new democratic order: in the glorious days of 1989, they equated democracy with the abundance of western consumerist societies; and 20 years later, with the abundance still missing, they now blame democracy itself.

Unfortunately, Dahrendorf focuses much less on the opposite temptation: if the majority resist the necessary structural changes in the economy, would one of the logical conclusions not be that, for a decade or so, an enlightened elite should take power, even by non-democratic means, to enforce the necessary measures and thus lay the foundations for truly stable democracy?

Along these lines, the journalist Fareed Zakaria pointed out how democracy can only 'catch on' in economically developed countries. If developing countries are 'prematurely democratised', the result is a populism that ends in economic catastrophe and political despotism – no wonder that today's economically most successful third world countries (Taiwan, South Korea, Chile) embraced full democracy only after a period of authoritarian rule. And, furthermore, does this line of thinking not provide the best argument for the authoritarian regime in China?

What is new today is that, with the financial crisis that began in 2008, this same distrust of democracy – once constrained to the third world or post-communist developing countries – is gaining ground in the developed west itself: what was a decade or two ago patronising advice to others now concerns ourselves.

The least one can say is that this crisis offers proof that it is not the people but experts themselves who do not know what they are doing. In Western Europe we are effectively witnessing a growing inability of the ruling elite – they know less and less how to rule. Look at how Europe is dealing with the Greek crisis: putting pressure on Greece to repay debts, but at the same time ruining its economy through imposed austerity measures and thereby making sure that the Greek debt will never be repaid.

At the end of October last year, the IMF itself released research showing that the economic damage from aggressive austerity measures may be as much as three times larger than previously assumed, thereby nullifying its own advice on austerity in the eurozone crisis. Now the IMF admits that forcing Greece and other debt-burdened countries to reduce their deficits too quickly would be counterproductive, but only after hundreds of thousands of jobs have been lost because of such 'miscalculations'.

And therein resides the true message of the 'irrational' popular protests all around Europe: the protesters know very well what they don't know; they don't pretend to have fast and easy answers; but what their instinct is telling them is nonetheless true – that those in power also don't know it. In Europe today, the blind are leading the blind.

SREĆKO HORVAT

4

WHY THE EU NEEDS CROATIA
MORE THAN CROATIA
NEEDS THE EU

When in late 2005 the accession negotiations between Croatia and the EU officially started, a leading Croatian liberal daily triumphantly published the following headline all over its front page: 'Bye, bye Balkans!' At that time, this was the prevailing and typical stance towards the European Union: some sort of 'self-fulfilling mythology' of the Balkans as a region needing to be 'civilised' by integration into the West. Only eight years later, as Croatia finally becomes part of the European Union, neither the EU nor the Balkans has the same image anymore. Today's situation is somehow reminiscent of the famous joke about a patient whose doctor makes him choose whether to hear the bad or the good news first. Of course, the patient chooses first to hear the bad news. 'The bad news is you have cancer,' says the doctor, 'but don't worry, the good news is you have Alzheimer's, so when you get home you will already have forgotten about the first predicament.' Doesn't that sound just like the situation with Croatia's EU accession, where the bad news is that Croatia is experiencing a political and economic crisis, with corruption affairs erupting almost on a daily basis and unemployment rates rising as well, and the good news is: 'Don't worry, you will enter the EU'?

'A clear majority in favour of EU accession' is how the teletext of the Austrian Broadcasting Corporation reported on the referendum in Croatia regarding the country's EU membership. And indeed, two-thirds of the votes cast said 'Yes'. But taking into account the historically low turnout in the referendum of 43 per cent, this means that actually not more than 29 per cent of the population entitled to vote spoke out in favour of EU accession. On the eve of Croatia's EU referendum, the former war general Ante Gotovina, recently released from his ICTY prison cell in The Hague, and who had once been the biggest obstacle to the Croatian negotiations with the EU, sent an epistle to the Croatian people urging them to vote in favour of the EU. At the same time, the two biggest Croatian parties, the Social Democrats (SDP), now in power, and the Conservatives (HDZ), the former ruling party, together with the Croatian Catholic Church, did everything to convince the voters that 'there is no alternative.'

Only a few days before the referendum, the foreign minister even went so far as to point out that pensions would not be paid unless the vote was 'Yes'. And, thanks to a 'Yes' campaign that cost around 600,000 euro, the main arguments were a similar type of 'blackmail alternative', among which the most frequent was: 'If we don't enter the EU, we will stay in the Balkans.' In such an atmosphere it is no surprise that the referendum on Croatia's accession to the EU recorded the lowest turnout among all current member states. With an attendance of only 43 per cent of its citizens, Croatia has beaten the previous record holder, Hungary, where the referendum was attended by 45 per cent. One possible explanation was nicely formulated by Croatia's prime minister after the first official results: 'Afraid that the referendum might fail, we changed the Constitution', involuntarily echoing the famous proverb by Bertolt Brecht: 'When government doesn't agree with the people, it's time to change the people.' Not only were the rules of the referendum indeed changed in 2010 because of the EU accession, but also other (legal, economic etc.) things were settled beforehand.

When, only six days after Mohamed Bouazizi's self-immolation which triggered the 'Arab Spring', 41-year-old TV engineer Adrian Sobaru attempted to commit suicide during the Romanian prime minister's speech in parliament by throwing himself off the gallery dressed in a T-shirt saying, 'You have killed our children's future! You sold us!' almost no-one took this as an indication of what was going to happen in the European Union. Only a year later, thousands of Romanians protested against austerity measures (mainly provoked by the privatisation of the healthcare system). Unlike at the time of the enlargement of the European Union in 2004 or 2007, there is no optimism in the air anymore – and yet, Croatia is joining the club.

Only last year the EU was facing huge protests and several general strikes from Spain, Portugal and Greece to England, Hungary, Romania and future member state Croatia.[13] And there is a new anti-democratic tendency in the EU, which does not only manifest itself in the success of right-wing movements (Golden Dawn, etc.) and governments (Viktor Orbán). An even bigger threat to democracy is the new technocrat elites in power; people who are actually provoking new nationalist tendencies and who all have one thing in common: they all worked for Goldman Sachs; people such as Mario Monti, Mario Draghi or Lucas Papademos. Actually, the last one is the best example for what is wrong with the EU today. If we play with the etymological meaning of 'papa' (which means 'father' and 'goodbye'), at the same time you have a 'father of the people' (Papa demos) and someone who is saying 'goodbye to the people' (Pa-pa demos). When we spoke about this weird congruity, Slavoj Žižek made a brilliant Hegelian synthesis: if you put the two together, you have neither more nor less than the mythology of Saturn who is eating all of its children, except Jupiter! (Namely, 'papa' in Croatian and Slovenian language also means 'eating'.)[14]

Actually, the Croatian referendum was another symptom of the EU's democratic deficit. We had a referendum after everything was already settled. We did not have a referendum in 2003, when Croatia applied for EU membership. We did not have a referendum in 2005, when Croatia officially opened negotiations with the EU. We did not even have a referendum in 2010, when our Constitution and the rules of the referendum were changed because of future EU membership. In other words, today we are in a situation where we can only choose what was already chosen throughout these stages. The question, repeated continuously by the Croatian government, 'What is the alternative?' already sounds like blackmail and is strangely reminiscent of the there-is-no-alternative-slogan made famous by Margaret Thatcher. And it is not by chance that we have a paradox here in the shape of an allegedly social-democratic government actually putting forward neoliberal reforms faster and more efficiently than the former con-servative government. Already now – as a plan to 'rescue' the economy – this social democratic government is announcing gradual privatisations of highways and railways, the energy sector and even prisons.

At the same time we witness the bizarre situation where the government is trying to convince the people that Croatia has to join the EU because, firstly, we will no longer be part of the Balkans anymore, and secondly, we will finally be part of the West. Sometimes it is enough to take a look at the path of the previous candidates who are now full members of the club, to see what sort of mythology haunts each new member state. In his provoking book *Eurosis – A critique of the new Eurocentrism*, Slovenian sociologist Mitja Velikonja made an extensive discourse analysis starting from the observation that the infinitely reproduced mantras of the new Eurocentric meta discourse have caught on and became normalised within all spheres of social life: in politics, in the media, in mass culture, in advertising, in everyday conversations. In his own words: 'Never during the one-party era of the uniformity of mind under Yugoslav totalitarianism did I see as many red communist stars as I saw yellow European stars in the spring of 2004, that is to say, under democracy.'[15] In short, what we have is a kind of 'virosis', therefore the neologism 'Eurosis'.

The pattern is always the same: according to the then Slovenian foreign minister, by joining the EU, Slovenia has come 'one step closer to the European centre, European trends, European life, European prosperity, European dynamics and the like'. On the other hand, all things that are 'backwards', 'bad' or 'out' stand for – you can guess – the Balkans. Or, as one journalist said in the Spanish daily El Pais, 'By joining the EU, Slovenia escaped the Balkan curse.' But if we take a closer look, Europe is 'Balkanised' already, and, on the other hand, the Balkans is 'Europeanised' as well. This can be best explained if we look at the main myths circulating in the Balkan region since Slovenia entered the EU and moving from one candidate to the other, finding its temporary resort in Croatia and waiting to transmigrate to other countries such as Montenegro or Serbia. The first myth is the one about corruption, the second on prosperity and the third brings us to the recent Nobel Peace Prize.

Here is the first myth: 'When we enter the EU, there will be less corruption.' By now, almost everyone knows about the Hollywood-like story of Croatian ex-Prime Minister Ivo Sanader, escaping from Croatia and being caught on the highway near Salzburg. He was accused of several corruption affairs, including an Austrian bank (Hypo-Alpe Adria) and Hungarian oil company (MOL). In other words, without European partners, he couldn't be involved in these corruption affairs. The last discovery is a 'deal' made between Sanader and Sarkozy, because of which Croatia's national carrier, Croatia Airlines, faces bankruptcy unless it can change a contract that was signed in 2008 by the former prime minister. Sanader struck a deal worth 135 million Euros with the former French president, to buy four planes back in 2008 with Airbus France. Croatia Airlines didn't really need the planes, but it was Sanader's ticket to secure a meeting with Sarkozy, just before France took over the presidency of the Council of the EU. At the same time, Jacques Chirac was found guilty of corruption and the German President Christian Wulff had to resign because of alleged corruption. So much about the thesis there will be less corruption in the EU than in the Balkans. What we are facing here is a clear case of applying double standards perfectly illustrated by a recent edition of the *Frankfurter Allgemeine Zeitung* where Commission President Barroso gave a big interview claiming we need 'more Europe', accompanied by a small piece of news that Romania won't get the green light to enter the Schengen Zone. Why? Because of corruption. So speaking about 'reforms' and 'monitoring', why isn't the same applied to the EU itself? And to take it to the extreme: why shouldn't new member states 'monitor' the EU?

And here we come to the second myth: 'When we enter the EU, there will be more prosperity.' It is not difficult to dispute this myth. It's enough to look at the 'prosperity' of PIIGS or, as they have recently been called, the GIPSI, an expression which, by the way, perfectly illustrates the actual significance of the periphery for the centre. Croatia will not join the centre

– it will be part of the GIPSI states. Recent statistics show that Croatia – with more than 50 per cent – is the third country in Europe when it comes to youth unemployment, after Greece and Spain. As the Polish philosopher Jaroslaw Makowski noticed, 'Until now, sociologists have focused on the so-called "lost generation", but politicians had been wary of using the phrase, until Italian Prime Minister Mario Monti broke the conspiracy of silence, telling his young compatriots: "You're a lost generation." Or, more precisely, "The truth, and unfortunately it's not a pleasant one, is that the promise of hope – in terms of transformation and improvement of the system – will be only for those young people who will come of age in a few years."'

Instead of precisely investing in young people, Monti even went so far to say that 'young people will have to get used to the idea of not having a fixed job for life', and added: 'which is moreover, monotonous! It is much nicer to change and accept new challenges'. So on the one hand, as Makowski explains, you have the 'enraged youth', which we saw in action in London's streets in summer 2011, the 'new poor' facing a prospect of protracted unemployment or flexi-jobs below their qualifications and ambitions, and on the other hand, although it is exactly the Erasmus generation that is Europe's last resort, education is being scrapped as part of 'austerity measures'.[16] Maybe the time has come to paraphrase the famous saying by Max Horkheimer and say, 'Anyone who does not wish to talk about neoliberalism, should also keep quiet on the subject of the EU.' And the same goes for 'reforms' in Croatia. Those who don't wish to talk about the reforms of the financial sector should also be quiet on the subject of all other (legal, human rights etc.) reforms. Already more than 90 per cent of banks in Croatia are Austrian, French, German or Italian, and the Croatian 'euro-compatible' elites are trying to implement further neoliberal reforms portrayed as a necessary part of the EU accession process. And maybe this is what Mr Barroso meant when he was saying that Croatia's accession to the EU will only strengthen the EU (with new privatisations and new capital flows).

The third myth linked with the myth of prosperity is the following: 'When we enter the EU, there will be more stability.' Or as one liberal Croatian intellectual put it before the referendum: 'For us the option is clear: either the Balkans or the civilised nations', and his colleague added: 'Eurosceptics are just bigoted obscurantists, maniacal patriots, fans of war criminals and tragicomic visionaries.' This is the old myth, reinforced for example by Emir Kusturica's movies, which show the Balkans as a dark region only good enough for war crimes. It is the 'Imaginary Balkans' so well explained in Maria Todorova's classic book under the same title. But when the European Union got the 2012 Nobel Peace Prize for having 'contributed to the advancement of peace and reconciliation, democracy and human rights in Europe', it was exactly this myth which was repeated in the official press release by the Norwegian selection committee: 'The admission of Croatia as a member next year, the opening of membership negotiations with Montenegro, and the granting of candidate status to Serbia all strengthen the process of reconciliation in the Balkans.' Here you have it again, a celebration of the European Union's mission 'civilisatrice', although it was exactly the EU that failed to stop massacres like that in Srebrenica. However, it is not really necessary to discredit the Nobel Peace Prize: by the time Henry Kissinger got it, it was obvious that Orwell's famous credo 'War is Peace' had become a new motto for its awarding, a suspicion confirmed by the choice of Obama, who afterwards did not withdraw his troops from either Iraq or Afghanistan. Nevertheless, it is necessary to mention that one of the prerequisites for joining the EU is to be a part of NATO, not really known for 'strengthening the process of reconciliation' if we have in mind the war in Libya or other places. Or take the recent war in Mali, where the EU is again sending troops to fight 'Islamic fundamentalism' under the pretext that it is endangering European democracy. It is also worth mentioning that the current presidency holder of the Council of the EU is Cyprus, a still divided country, and that the Nobel Peace Prize is given in a country whose citizens twice refused EU membership. All in all, the myth of 'stability' goes hand in hand with the myth of 'prosperity', as there is no real peace in Europe, but exactly the opposite – a permanent economic warfare going on in the 'bay of PIIGS'. Is there any better proof than the submarine deals that helped sink Greece, the billions spent on buying German U-boats while the EU is pushing for deeper cuts in areas like health or education?

So maybe the time has come to change the doctor joke and switch the roles. The bad news is that the EU is in a big political and economic crisis, with corruption affairs erupting almost on a daily basis and unemployment rates rising. The good news is that Croatia is entering the EU: it is precisely Croatia's accession, just like the Nobel Peace Prize, that should give new credibility and legitimacy to the European Union in its current state. In that sense, we could say that at this moment the EU needs Croatia more than Croatia needs Europe in the state it is currently in.

Slavoj Žižek

5

WHAT DOES EUROPE WANT?

On 1 May 2004, eight new countries were welcomed into the European Union – but which 'Europe' will they find there? In the months before Slovenia's entry to the European Union, whenever a foreign journalist asked me what new dimension Slovenia would contribute to Europe, my answer was instant and unambiguous: *nothing*. Slovene culture is obsessed with the notion that, although a small nation, we are a cultural superpower: We possess some 'agalma', a hidden intimate treasure of cultural masterpieces that wait to be acknowledged by the wider world. Maybe this treasure is too fragile to survive intact the exposure to the fresh air of international competition, like the old Roman frescoes in that wonderful scene from Fellini's *Roma*, which start to dissolve the moment that daylight reaches them.

Such narcissism is not a Slovene speciality. There are versions of it all around Eastern Europe: we value democracy more because we had to fight for it recently, not being allowed to take it for granted; we still know what true culture is, not being corrupted by the cheap Americanised mass culture. Rejecting such a fixation on the hidden national treasure in no way implies ethnic self-hatred. The point is a simple and cruel one: all Slovene artists who made a relevant contribution had to 'betray' their ethnic roots at some point, either by isolating themselves from the cultural mainstream in Slovenia or by simply leaving the country for some time, living in Vienna or Paris. It is the same as with Ireland: not only did James Joyce leave home in order to write *Ulysses*, his masterpiece about Dublin; Yeats himself, the poet of Irish national revival, spent years in London. The greatest threats to national tradition are its local guardians who warn about the danger of foreign influences. Furthermore, the Slovene attitude of cultural superiority finds its counterpart in the patronising Western cliché which characterises the East European post-communist countries as retarded poor cousins who will be admitted back into the family if they can behave properly. Recall the reaction of the press to the last elections in Serbia where the nationalists gained votes – it was read as a sign that Serbia is not yet ready for Europe.

A similar process is going on now in Slovenia: the fact that nationalists collected enough signatures to enforce a referendum about the building of a mosque in Ljubljana is sad enough; the fact that the majority of the population thinks that one should not allow the mosque is even sadder; and the arguments evoked (should we allow our beautiful countryside to be spoiled by a minaret that stands for fundamentalist barbarism? etc.) make one ashamed of being a Slovene. In such cases, the occasional threats from Brussels can only appear welcome: show multiculturalist tolerance ... or else! However, this simplified picture is not the entire truth. The first complication: the very ex-communist countries which are the most ardent supporters of the US 'war on terror' deeply worry that their cultural identity, their very survival as nations, is threatened by the onslaught of cultural 'Americanisation' as the price for their immersion into global capitalism.

We thus witness the paradox of pro-Bushist anti-American-ism. In Slovenia, the Rightist nationalists complain that the ruling Centre-Left coalition, though it is publicly for joining NATO and supporting the US anti-terrorist campaign, is secretly sabotaging it, participating in it for opportunist reasons and not from conviction. At the same time, however, it reproaches the ruling coalition for undermining Slovene national identity by advocating full Slovene integration into the Westernised global capitalism and thus drowning Slovenes in contemporary Americanised pop culture. The idea is that the ruling coalition sustains pop culture, stupid TV amusement and mindless consumption in order to turn Slovenes into an easily manipulated crowd, incapable of serious reflection and firm ethical stances. In short, the underlying motif is that the ruling coalition stands for the 'liberal-communist plot': ruthless, unconstrained immersion in global capitalism is perceived as the latest dark plot of the ex-communists, enabling them to retain their secret hold on power. Ironically, the nationalist conservatives' lament about the new emerging socio-ideological order reads like the old New Left's description of the 'repressive tolerance' of capitalist freedom as the mode of unfreedom's appearance.

This ambiguity of the Eastern European attitude finds its perfect counterpart in the ambiguous message of the West to post-communist countries. Recall the two-sided pressure the United States exerted on Serbia in the summer of 2003: US representatives simultaneously demanded that Serbia deliver the suspected war criminals to the Hague court (in accordance with the logic of the global Empire which demands a trans-state global judicial institution) AND to sign the bilateral treaty with the United States obliging Serbia not to deliver to any international institution (i.e., the SAME Hague court) US citizens suspected of war crimes or other crimes against humanity (in accordance with the Nation-State logic). No wonder the Serb reaction is one of perplexed fury! And a similar thing is going on at the economic level: while pressuring Poland to open its agriculture to market competition, Western Europe floods the Polish market with agricultural products heavily subsidised from Brussels. How do post-communist countries navigate in this sea with conflicting winds? If there is an ethical hero of the recent time in ex-Yugoslavia, it is Ika Šarić, a modest judge in Croatia who, in the face of threats to her life and without any visible public support, condemned General Mirko Norac and his colleagues to 12 years in prison for the crimes committed in 1992 against the Serb civilian population. Even the Leftist government, afraid of the threat of the Rightist nationalist demonstrations, refused to stand firmly behind the trial against Norac.

However, just as the nationalist Right was intimating that large public disorders would topple the government, when the sentence was proclaimed, *nothing happened*. The demonstrations were much smaller than expected and Croatia 'rediscovered' itself as a state of the rule of law. It was especially important that Norac was not delivered to the Hague, but condemned in Croatia itself – Croatia thus proved that it does not need international tutelage. The dimension of the act proper consisted in the shift from the impossible to the possible: before the sentence, the nationalist Right with its veteran organisations was perceived as a powerful force not to be provoked, and the direct harsh sentence was perceived by the liberal Left as something that 'we all want, but, unfortunately, cannot afford in this difficult moment, since chaos would ensue'. However, after the sentence was proclaimed and nothing happened, the impossible turned into the routine. If there is any dimension to be redeemed of the signifier 'Europe', then this act was 'European' in the most exemplary sense of the term. And if there is an event that embodies the cowardice, it is the behaviour of the Slovene government after the outbreak of the Iraq-US war. Slovene politicians desperately tried to steer a middle course between US pressure and the unpopularity of the war with the majority of the Slovene population. First, Slovenia signed the infamous Vilnius declaration for which it was praised by Rumsfeld and others as part of the 'new Europe' of the 'coalition of the willing' in the war against Iraq. However, after the foreign minister signed the document, there ensued a true comedy of denials: the minister claimed that, before signing the document, he consulted the president of the republic and other dignitaries, who promptly denied that they knew anything about it; then, all concerned claimed that the document in no way supported the unilateral US attack on Iraq, but called for the key role of the United Nations. The specification was that Slovenia supported the disarmament of Iraq, but not the war on Iraq. However, a couple of days later, there was a bad surprise from the United States: Slovenia was not only explicitly named among the countries participating in the 'coalition of the willing' but was even designated as the recipient of financial aid from the United States to its war partners. What ensued was pure comedy: Slovenia proudly declared that it did not participate in the war against Iraq and demanded to be struck from the list. After a couple of days, a new embarrassing document was received: the United States officially thanked Slovenia for its support and help. Slovenia again protested that it did not qualify for any thanks and refused to recognise itself as the proper addressee of the letter, in a kind of mocking version of 'Please, I do not really deserve your thanks!', as if sending its thanks was the worst thing the United States could do to us. Usually, states protest when they are unjustly criticised; Slovenia protests when it receives signs of gratitude.

In short, Slovenia behaved as if it was not the proper recipient of the letters of praise that went on and on – and what we all knew was that, in this case also, the letter *did* arrive at its proper destination. The ambiguity of Eastern Europeans therefore merely mirrors the inconsistencies of Western Europe itself.

Late in his life, Freud asked the famous question, 'Was will das Weib?' ('What does Woman want?'), admitting his perplexity when faced with the enigma of feminine sexuality. And a similar perplexity arises today, when post-communist countries are entering the European Union: which Europe will they be entering? For long years, I have been pleading for a renewed 'Leftist Eurocentrism'. To put it bluntly, do we want to live in a world in which the only choice is between the American civilisation and the emerging Chinese authoritarian-capitalist one? If the answer is no, then the only alternative is Europe. The Third World cannot generate a strong enough resistance to the ideology of the American Dream; in the present constellation, it is only Europe that can do it. The true opposition today is not the one between the First World and the Third World, but the one between the Whole of the First and Third World (the American global Empire and its colonies) and the remaining Second World (Europe). Apropos Freud, Theodor Adorno claimed that what we are getting in our contemporary 'administered world' and its 'repressive desubli-mation' is no longer the old logic of repression of the id and its drives, but a perverse direct pact between the punitive superego and the id's illicit aggressive drives at the expense of the ego's rational agency. Is not something structurally similar going on today at the political level, the weird pact between the post-modern global capitalism and the pre-modern societies at the expense of modernity proper? It is easy for the American multiculturalist global Empire to integrate pre-modern local traditions – the foreign body that it effectively cannot assimilate is European modernity. Jihad and McWorld are two sides of the same coin. Jihad is already McJihad. Although the ongoing 'war on terror' presents itself as the defence of the democratic legacy, it courts the danger clearly perceived a century ago by G.K. Chesterton who, in his Orthodoxy, deployed the fundamental deadlock of the critics of religion: 'Men who begin to fight the Church for the sake of freedom and humanity end by flinging away freedom and humanity if only they may fight the Church ... The secularists have not wrecked divine things; but the secularists have wrecked secular things, if that is any comfort to them.' Does the same not hold today for the advocates of religion themselves? How many fanatical defenders of religion started by ferociously attacking the contemporary secular culture and ended up forsaking any meaningful religious experience? In a similar way, many liberal warriors are so eager to fight anti-democratic fundamentalism that they will end by flinging away freedom and democracy themselves if only they may fight terror. They have such a passion for proving that non-Christian fundamentalism is the main threat to freedom that they are ready to fall back on the position that we have to limit our own freedom here and now, in our allegedly Christian societies. If the 'terrorists' are ready to wreck this world for love of another world, our warriors on terror are ready to wreck their own democratic world out of hatred for the Muslim other. Some of them love human dignity so much that they are ready to legalise torture – the ultimate degradation of human dignity – to defend it. And, along the same lines, we may lose 'Europe' through its very defence.

A year ago, an ominous decision of the European Union passed almost unnoticed: the plan to establish an all-European border police force to secure the isolation of the

Union territory and thus to prevent the influx of immigrants. *This* is the truth of globalisation: the construction of *new* walls safeguarding the prosperous Europe from the immigrant flood. One is tempted to resuscitate here the old Marxist 'humanist' opposition of 'relations between things' and 'relations between persons': in the much-celebrated free circulation opened up by global capitalism, it is 'things' (commodities) which freely circulate, while the circulation of 'persons' is more and more controlled. This new racism of the developed is in a way much more brutal than the racism of the past: its implicit legitimisation is neither naturalist (the 'natural' superiority of the developed West) nor any longer culturalist (we in the West also want to preserve our cultural identity), but unabashed economic egotism – the funda-mental divide is between those included in the sphere of (relative) economic prosperity and those excluded from it. What we find reprehensible and dangerous in US politics and civilisation is thus *a part of Europe itself,* one of the possible outcomes of the European project. There is no place for self-satisfied arrogance: the United States is a distorted mirror of Europe itself. Back in the 1930s, Max Horkheimer wrote that those who do not want to speak (critically) about liberalism should also keep silent about fascism. *Mutatis mutandis,* one should say to those who decry the new US imperialism: those who do not want to engage critically with Europe itself should also keep silent about the United States. This, then, is the only true question beneath the self-congratulatory celebrations that accompany the extension of the European Union: *what* Europe are we joining? And when confronted with this question, all of us, 'New' and 'Old' Europe, are in the same boat.

SREĆKO HORVAT

6

ARE THE NAZIS LIVING
ON THE MOON?

Recently in Bucharest, I came across an apparently innocent map of seminar rooms in the lift of the hotel where the conference on 'The National Question in Central-Eastern Europe' was taking place. There it was, a little map of Europe, consisting of 'Berlin room', 'Amsterdam room', 'Paris room', 'London room', and others, promoting the diversity but at the same time unity of the European project. Is there a better imagining of the solved national question in the European Union? All countries living beside one another, happily and without conflict, each room with its own identity and activity; in one room a wedding party, in another an academic conference, in one a commercial promotion of a given product, in some other a focus group, and so on. And what is even better, you don't even have to leave the hotel – everything is here.

Maybe the answer is given by another odd example, that of *Costa Concordia*, the famous cruise ship that hit a rock in the Tyrrhenian Sea in January 2012. Its name ('Concordia') symbolised the harmony and unity between European nations, and the ship – just like the seminar rooms in the Romanian hotel – was comprised of 13 decks named after EU member states: Poland was the upper deck, followed by Austria, Portugal, Spain, Germany, France, etc. In the middle of the ship there was an 'Atrium Europe' with a 'London Salon', 'Disco Lisbon', 'Berlin bar', etc. It's hard not to take into account the fact that *Costa Concordia* served as the setting for Jean-Luc Godard's *Socialism*, which took it as a symbol for modern Europe – not a warship, or a speedboat, but a slow, huge, luxurious cruiser. For example, in the film, Alain Badiou is holding a lecture in front of an empty hall, and Patti Smith is wandering the decks with her guitar ... but, no-one really cares.

So, in a way, retroactively, the decks of *Costa Concordia* named after European countries and Godard's last film give us a possible picture of today's Europe. There is no real harmony and unity, just decay that inevitably leads to a disaster. Isn't the captain of *Costa Concordia*, who, the night before the accident, was spending his time in the company of beautiful women drinking expensive wine, also a metaphor of the current financial elites of Europe? Isn't the captain who left the ship before his passengers similar to those bankers, managers and brokers from Goldman Sachs and the European Central Bank, who always leave the sinking boat on time, leaving the people to drown like they do today in Greece or elsewhere in Southern Europe? On the one hand, the European central bank 'released' more than 1,000 billion Euros from December 2011, but not to save the people, but to again save the banks. On the other hand, we bear witness to a continuing of the shock therapy of austerity measures and structural adjustments in all European countries, from Greece and Romania, from Italy and Spain, and also Slovenia and Croatia.

One of the consequences of this radical neoliberal turn is the rise of the extreme right and nationalism, which are increasingly mobilising the working class. It's not by chance that the name of the extreme right party in the Czech Republic, infamous for organising pogroms against Roma people, is the 'Workers Party'. As it shouldn't surprise us that the biggest surprise of the last Greek elections wasn't only SYRIZA, but the Golden Dawn, previously a marginal pro-fascist group that blames immigrants for bringing Greece into the crisis and for 'stealing' the jobs of ordinary Greeks during the crisis.[17] In short, as a result of the financial crisis, the right and the extreme right camp are getting more and more powerful.

Here is a typical illustration of this rhetoric: 'They have taken all our sovereign rights from us. We are just good enough for international capital to allow us to fill its money sacks with interest payments ... Three million people lack work and sustenance. The officials, it is true, work to conceal the misery. They speak of measures and silver linings. Things are getting steadily better for them, and steadily worse for us. The illusion of freedom, peace and prosperity that we were promised when we wanted to take our fate into our own hands is vanishing. Only the complete collapse of our people can follow from these irresponsible policies.'

Isn't this a perfect description of Europe's current dead-lock? Would you expect such a discourse from SYRIZA or from the Golden Dawn? The answer might be surprising: the author is no-one else than Joseph Goebbels, and it's part of his text 'Wir fordern' ('We demand') published in the fourth issue of *Der Angriff*, dated 25 July 1927.[18] At first, this was a marginal newspaper using the motto 'For the oppressed against the exploiters', and then, in 1933, it turned into the 'Daily Newspaper of the German Labour Front'. In 1927, the circulation was around 2,000. In 1933, it was almost 150,000 and in 1944 around 306,000.[19] What should not surprise us – but at the same time warn us – is the discourse ('we are just good enough for international capital to allow us to fill its money sacks with interest payments') and the reference to the working class (the 'official' newspaper of the 'Labour Front'). Just like the Golden Dawn at its inception, it was a completely irrelevant and ridiculous group of lunatics trying to use the financial crisis to gain support, yet step by step it turned into a powerful weapon of a totalitarian vision of Europe.

Regardless of all political and economical parallels and predispositions between the financial crisis of 2008 and the crisis of 1929, we have to be careful when comparing the present-day situation to the historical moment when the Nazis came to power. Nevertheless, it might well be dangerous to dismiss the fact that, hand in hand with the current financial crisis, the right camp has once again raised the national question in order to divert attention from the real political, social and economic situation. Here a comic science-fiction film called *Iron Sky* (Timo Vuorensola, 2012) could give us an unexpected lesson. It tells the story of Nazis who, after being defeated in 1945, fled to the Moon, where they built a space fleet with which to return to conquer Earth in 2018. At first, in the lead-up to 'The Final Solution', two Nazis arrive on Earth in order to check that everything is ready, but no-one believes them. Until their potential is discovered by a campaign manager who is desperately trying to figure out a presidential campaign for a politician who is an unambiguous parody of Sarah Palin. She realises that the phraseology and discourse of the Nazis is exactly what can be sold during the crisis and can be used as a perfect tool for attracting more voters. In the end, when it's already too late, she finds out that the Nazis are really Nazis and that what they really want is to conquer Earth.

This brings us back to today's predicament. In the late

1920s, gas chambers and all the atrocities performed by Nazis probably also seemed to be a science-fiction scenario, like an invasion of Nazis from the Moon does today. But if the comparison between Goebbels' discourse and contemporary extreme right tendencies looks like an exaggerated comparison, let me point to a recent 'experiment' by two young unemployed Serbian playwrights who wanted to prove that it is possible to unite all political parties in Serbia using one of Goebbels' texts. In April 2012, applying for membership in the main Serbian parties, they sent a policy proposal for cultural politics in Serbia under the title 'Idea, Strategy, Movement'. Their text and vision was very well accepted by all parties and they were immediately granted membership and were offered positions after the elections. What they did was very simple: they just used Goebbels' text 'Knowledge and Propaganda' from 1928, changed a few sentences and applied it to the Serbian context. One political party even published the text on its official website.

About the same time when the Serbian playwrights succeeded in proving that it was possible to effectively use Goebbels' propaganda today, a Croatian extreme right party tried to organise an international meeting of nationalists in Zagreb. Among others, the invited parties included the National Democratic Party from Germany, linked to the recent Neo-Nazi murders there; the National Front from France, infamous for denying the Holocaust; and last but not least, the Hungarian Jobbik, which is probably the most bizarre component of the story: namely, Jobbik tries to come up with a revision of the Trianon Treaty of 1920 which caused Hungary to lose its territories, including some parts of Croatia. So, you have a situation where Croatian nationalists are inviting Hungarian nationalists who want to see a big part of Croatian territory reincorporated into Greater Hungary!

But it would be wrong to only laugh at these far-right absurdities. What was the first thing the Austrian politician Hans Christian Strache, infamous author of the slogans 'Mehr Mut für unser Wiener Blutt' ('More courage for Vienna's blood') and 'Fremdes tut niemanden gut' ('Foreign is no good') did after he won 26 per cent at the Vienna elections in 2010? Together with other extremists he went for a 'team building' retreat, not to the Reichstadt but to Israel, in order to build stronger connections with the ones who were once Hitler's foremost enemies and victims. Furthermore, in December 2010, they issued the 'Jerusalem Declaration', which affirmed Israel's right to exist and defend itself against Islamic terror. And, at Strache's invitation, Israeli Deputy Minister Ayoob Kara subsequently visited Vienna.[20]

And what is even more interesting, is that the strongest allies Strache had in Vienna were the growing Serbian immigrant community. In order to get rid of the unwanted immigrants such as Africans, Turks and generally the Muslim population, one creates 'good' immigrants, in this case the Serbs. And it shouldn't surprise us that one of the inspirations for Anders Breivik was none other than the Serbian war criminal, Radovan Karadžić. As he says in his Manifesto *2083 – A European Declaration of Independence*: 'I do condemn any atrocities committed against Croats and vice versa but for his efforts to purge Serbia of Islam he will always be considered and remembered as an honourable Crusader and a European war hero.'[21] So, what appears today is a new kind of extreme right that doesn't hesitate to use all possible means in order to build a stronger movement. And instead of easily dismissing these absurd alliances, here we should remind ourselves of Walter Benjamin's important lesson that 'Every fascism bears witness to a failed revolution.'

As we can see, the situation produced by ongoing financial

crisis and imposed austerity measures is a fertile ground not only for a new accumulation of capital by the financial elites, but also for the rise of new nationalisms. Using workers' rights as the main weapon is not only the means of the Left anymore. The difference between the Right and between the Left is, nevertheless, clear: the Right is turning one working class against the other (the German against the Greek, the Austrian and the Greek against the immigrants, and so on), and uses the 'workers' discourse' mainly to finally grab power. But former marginal and extremist groups are now becoming not only legitimate, but also legal parties. The Golden Dawn is not an exception anymore, but a rule. The Nazis don't have to hide on the dark side of the Moon – they can calmly live on the Earth, undisturbed. And what is needed now isn't only SYRIZA, but a united and strong European Left.

Slavoj Žižek

7

THE RETURN OF THE CHRISTIAN-CONSERVATIVE REVOLUTION

The German expression *'rückgängig machen'*, usually translated as 'annul, cancel, unhitch', has a more precise connotation: to retroactively undo something, to make it as if it didn't take place. The comparison between Mozart's *Figaro* and Rossini's *Figaro*-operas makes this immediately clear. In Mozart, the emancipatory political potential of Beaumarchais's play survives the pressure of censorship – think only of the finale, where the Count has to kneel down and ask for forgiveness of his subjects (not to mention the explosion of the collective *'Viva la libertà!'* in the finale of Act 1 of *Don Giovanni*). The breathtaking achievement of Rossini's *Barber* should be measured by this standard: Rossini took a theatrical piece which was one of THE symbols of the French bourgeois revolutionary spirit, and totally de-politicised it, changing it into a pure opera buffa. No wonder the golden years of Rossini were 1815–1830: the years of reaction, the years in which the European powers tackled the impossible task of the *'Ungeschehenmachen'* (making-it-not-happen) of the previous revolutionary decades. This is what Rossini did in his great comic operas: they try to bring back to life the innocence of the pre-revolutionary world. Rossini did not actively hate and fight against the new world – he simply composed as if the years 1789–1815 didn't exist. Rossini was therefore right to (almost) stop composing after 1830 and to adopt the satisfied stance of a bon vivant making his 'tournedos' – this was the only properly ethical thing to do, and his long silence is comparable to that of Jan Sibelius (and, in literature, to those of Arthur Rimbaud and Dashiell Hammett).

In so far as the French Revolution is THE Event of modern history, the break after which 'nothing was the same', one should raise here the question: is this kind of 'undoing', of 'dis-eventalisation', one of the possible destinies of every Event? It is possible to imagine the attitude of the fetishist split towards an Event: 'I know very well there was no Event, just the ordinary run of things, but, perhaps, unfortunately, nonetheless ... (I believe) there WAS one'? And, an even more interesting case, is it possible for an Event to be not directly denied but denied retroactively? Imagine a society which fully integrated into its ethical substance the great modern axioms of freedom, equality, democratic rights, the duty of a society to provide for education and basic healthcare of all its members. This society also rendered racism and sexism simply unacceptable and ridiculous, so that there is no need even to argue against, say, racism, since anyone who openly advocates racism is immediately perceived as a weird eccentric who cannot be taken seriously, etc. But then, step by step, although a society continues to pay lip service to these axioms, they are de facto deprived of their substance. Here is an example from ongoing European history: in the summer of 2012, Viktor Orban, the Hungarian Rightist PM, said that in Central Europe a new economic system must be built:

And let us hope that God will help us and we will not have to invent a new type of political system instead of this democracy that must be introduced for the sake of economic survival ... Cooperation is a question of force, not of intention. Perhaps there are countries where things don't work that way, for example in the Scandinavian countries, but such a half-Asiatic rag-tag people as we are can unite only if we are forced to.[22]

The irony of these lines was not lost on some old Hungarian dissidents: when the Soviet army moved into Budapest to crush the 1956 anti-communist uprising, the message repeatedly sent by the beleaguered Hungarian leaders to the West was: 'We are defending Europe here.' (against the Asiatic communists, of course). Now, after communism has collapsed, the Christian-conservative government paints Western multicultural consumerist liberal democracy as its main enemy – this being exactly what today's Western Europe stands for – and calls for a new, more organic communitarian order to replace the 'turbulent' liberal democracy of the last two decades. In the latest instalment of the saga of designating the Enemy as the coincidence of opposites ('plutocratic-Bolshevik plot', etc.), (ex-) communists and liberal 'bourgeois' democrats are perceived as two faces of the same enemy. No wonder Orban and some of his allies repeatedly express their sympathies for the Chinese version of 'capitalism with Asian values'; looking to 'Asian' authoritarianism as the solution against the ex-communist threat.

But we should approach this topic gradually, in a more systematic way, beginning with the obscene underside of a post-evental reality which undoes itself from within. According to legend, Alfred Hitchcock (himself a Catholic) was once driving through a small Swiss town; all of a sudden, he pointed his finger at something through the car window and said: 'This is the most terrifying scene I've ever seen!' A friend sitting at his side looked in the direction pointed at by Hitchcock with surprise: there was nothing outstanding out there, just a priest who, while talking to a young boy, put his hand onto the boy's arm. Hitchcock halted the car, rolled down the window and shouted: 'Run, boy, save your life!' While this anecdote could be taken as a display of Hitchcock's eccentric showmanship, it does bring us to the 'heart of darkness' of the Catholic Church.

We recall numerous cases of paedophilia that have shocked the Catholic Church: when its representatives insist that these cases, deplorable as they are, are the church's internal problem, and display great reluctance to collaborate with police in their investigation. In a way, they are right – the paedophilia of Catholic priests is not something that concerns merely the persons who, due to incidental reasons of private history which bear no relation to the church as an institution, happened to choose the profession of a priest; it is a phenomenon that concerns the Catholic Church in that it is inscribed into its very functioning as a socio-symbolic institution. It does not concern the 'private' unconscious of individuals, but the 'unconscious' of the institution itself: it is not something that happens because the institution has to accommodate itself to the pathological realities of libidinal life in order to survive, but something that the institution itself needs in order to reproduce itself. One can well imagine a 'straight' (that is, not paedophiliac) priest who, after years of service, gets involved in paedophilia because the very logic of the institution seduces him into it. Such an institutional unconscious designates the obscene, disavowed underside that, precisely because it is disavowed, sustains the public institution. (In the army, this underside consists of the obscene sexualised rituals of fragging, etc. which sustain the group solidarity.) In other words, it is not simply that, for conformist reasons, the church tries to hush up embarrassing paedophilic scandals; in defending itself, the church defends its innermost obscene secret. What this means is that identifying oneself with this secret side is a key constituent of the very identity of a Christian priest: if a priest seriously (not just rhetorically) denounces these scandals, he thereby excludes himself from the ecclesiastic community, he is no longer 'one of us' (in exactly the same way a citizen of a town in the South of the US in the 1920s, if he denounced the Ku Klux Klan to the police, excluded himself from his community, and therefore betrayed its fundamental solidarity). Consequently, the answer to the church's reluctance should result in the realisation that we are dealing with criminal cases and that, if the church does not fully participate in their investigation, it is an accomplice after the fact; and moreover, the church AS SUCH, as an institution, should be investigated with regard to the way it systematically creates conditions for such crimes. That is to say, what makes these crimes so disturbing is that they did not just happen in religious surroundings but that these surroundings were part of them; directly mobilised as the instrument of seduction:

> ... the seduction technique employs religion. Almost always some sort of prayer has been used as foreplay. The very places where the molestation occurs are redolent of religion – the sacristy, the confessional, the rectory, Catholic schools and clubs with sacred pictures on the walls ... a conjunction of the over-strict sexual instruction of the Church (e.g., on the mortal sinfulness of masturbation, when even one occurrence of which can, if not confessed, send one to hell) and a guide who can free one of inexplicably dark teaching by inexplicably

sacred exceptions ...The predator ...uses religion to sanction
what he is up to, when calling sex part of his priestly ministry.[23]

Religion is not just invoked in order to provide a frisson of
the forbidden, i.e. to heighten the pleasure by making sex an
act of transgression; on the contrary, sex itself is presented in
religious terms, as the religious cure for the sin (of
masturbation). The paedophilic priests were not liberals who
seduced boys by claiming that gay sexuality is healthy and
permitted – in a masterful use of the reversal which Lacan
calls 'point de capiton', they first insisted that the confessed
sin of a boy (masturbation) really is mortal, and then they
offered gay acts (say, mutual masturbation) – i.e. something
that cannot but appear as an even GREATER sin – as a
'healing' procedure. The key resides in this mysterious 'tran-
substantiation' by means of which the prohibiting Law which
makes us feel guilty apropos an ordinary sin is enacted in
the guise of a much greater sin – as if, in a kind of Hegelian
coincidence of the opposites, the Law coincides with the
greatest transgression. Therefore is the present US politics,
in its inherent structure, not a kind of political equivalent of
the Catholic paedophilia? The problem of its new moral
vigour is not just that morality is manipulatively exploited,
but that it is directly mobilised; the problem with its appeal
to democracy is that it is not simply hypocrisy and external
manipulation, but that it directly mobilises and relies on
'sincere' democratic strivings.

In the summer of 2012, there occurred in Slovenia an
almost clinically pure display of the Catholic Church's
obscenity. It involved two actors, the conservative Cardinal
Franc Rode, a Slovene with a place in the highest ranks of the
Church nomenclature, and Alojz Uran, the arch-bishop who
was first deposed by the Vatican and then even ordered to

immediately leave Slovenia until accusations against him were clarified. Since Uran was very popular among ordinary Catholic believers, rumours started to circulate about the reasons for this extraordinarily harsh punishment. After a week or so of embarrassing silence, the Church authorities grudgingly proclaimed that Uran was suspected of fathering an illegitimate child – an explanation which, for a series of reasons, was met with widespread disbelief. Firstly, rumours about Uran's claimed paternity had already been circulating for decades, so why had the Church not taken measures years before when Uran was nominated the arch-bishop of Slovenia? Secondly, Uran himself publicly proclaimed that he was ready to undergo a DNA, or any other, test in order to prove that he has no children. Last but not least, it is well-known that, in the Slovene Church, a long struggle had been going on between Conservatives (among them Rode) and moderates (among them Uran). But whatever the truth, the public was shocked by the double standards displayed by the Catholic nomenclature: while Uran was ordered to leave Slovenia due to the mere suspicion of fathering a child, the reaction of the Church was infinitely more soft in regards to the numerous cases of paedophilia among the priests – the cases were never reported to the police; the responsible priest was never punished but just moved to another part of Slovenia; there was pressure on the parents of the abused children to keep things under the carpet, etc.[24]

What made things even worse, was the open cynical 'realism' displayed by Cardinal Rode: in one of his radio interviews, he said that 'statistically, this is an irrelevant problem – one or at the utmost two out of hundred priests had this kind of adventure.' What immediately drew the attention of the public was the term 'kind of adventure' being used as an euphemism for paedophilia: the brutal crime of raping children was thus presented as a normal display of adventurous 'vivacity' (another term used by Rode), and, as Rode quipped in another interview: 'Over forty years, you would expect some small sins to occur, wouldn't you?' This is Catholic obscenity at its purest: instead of solidarity with the victims (the children), what we find beneath the morally upright posture is simply the barely concealed solidarity with the perpetrators in the name of cynical realism (that's how life is, we are all red under our skin, and priests can also be adventurous and vivacious). So in the end, the only true victims appear to be the Church and the perpetrators who themselves have been exposed to an unfair media campaign. The lines are thus clearly drawn: paedophilia is ours, our own dirty secret, and as such normalised, the secret foundation of our normality, while fathering a child is a true violation to be ruthlessly rejected. A century ago, G.K.Chesterton summed it up in his book, *Orthodoxy* (unaware of the full consequences of his words, of course):

> The outer ring of Christianity is a rigid guard of ethical abnegations and professional priests; but inside that inhuman guard you will find the old human life dancing like children, and drinking wine like men; for Christianity is the only frame for pagan freedom.

The perverse conclusion is unavoidable here: do you want to enjoy the pagan dream of pleasurable life without paying the price of melancholic sadness for it? Choose Christianity! We can discern the traces of this paradox in the well-known Catholic figure of the Priest (or Nun) as the ultimate bearer of sexual wisdom. Recall what is arguably the most powerful scene of *The Sound of Music*: after Maria escapes from the von Trapp family back to the monastery, unable to deal with her sexual attraction towards Baron von Trapp, she cannot find peace there, since she is still longing for the Baron. In a memorable scene, the Mother Superior summons her and advises her to return to the von Trapp family and try to sort out her relationship with the Baron. She delivers this message in a weird song, entitled 'Climb every mountain!', whose surprising motif is: Do it! Take the risk and try everything your heart wants! Do not allow petty considerations to stand in your way! The uncanny power of this scene resides in its unexpected display of the spectacle of desire, which renders the scene literally embarrassing: the very person whom one would expect to preach abstinence and renunciation turns out to be the agent of fidelity to one's desire.

Significantly, when *The Sound of Music* was shown in (still Socialist) Yugoslavia in the late 1960s, THIS scene – the three minutes of this song – was the only part of the film which was censored (cut out). The anonymous Socialist censor thereby displayed his profound sense for the truly dangerous power of Catholic ideology: far from being the religion of sacrifice, of renunciation to earthly pleasures (in contrast to the pagan affirmation of the life of passions), Christianity offers a devious stratagem to indulge in our desires WITHOUT HAVING TO PAY THE PRICE FOR THEM; to enjoy life without the fear of decay and debilitating pain awaiting us at the end of the day. If we continue in this direction to the end, it would even be possible to sustain that therein resides the ultimate function of Christ's sacrifice: you can indulge in your desires and enjoy, because I took the price for it upon myself! In the perverse functioning of Christianity, religion is effectively evoked as a safeguard allowing us to enjoy life with impunity. Indeed, Lacan was right in turning around Dostoyevsky's well-known dictum: If there is God, then everything is permitted. Today, with the ever-growing number of cases of paedophilia in the

Catholic Church, one can easily imagine a new version of the scene from *The Sound of Music*: a young priest approaches the abbot, complaining that he is still tortured by desires for young boys, and demanding further punishment; the abbot answers by singing 'Climb every young boy ...'

One has to draw a further distinction here; between adult male homosexuality and paedophilia. Recent outbursts of homophobia in East European post-communist states should give us pause to think: in the gay parades which took place in recent years in Serbia and Croatia (in the cities of Belgrade and Split), the police were not able to protect participants who were ferociously attacked by thousands of violent Christian fundamentalists – how can one understand this wrath alongside the fact that the main force behind the anti-gay movement in Croatia is the Catholic Church, which is now well-known for its numerous paedophilic scandals? (A Croat gay activist sarcastically remarked that the error of the gays is that their partners are adult men and not children.) It can be helpful to draw a parallel here with the army, another type of organised crowd mentioned by Freud in the same group with the church. From my own experience of military service in 1975, I remember the old, infamous Yugoslav People's Army being homophobic in the extreme – when someone was discovered to have homosexual inclinations, he was instantly turned into a pariah, treated as a non-person, and then formally dismissed from the Army. Yet, at the same time, everyday army life was excessively permeated with the atmosphere of homosexual innuendos[25]. How is this weird coincidence of the opposites possible? The mechanism was described by Robert Pfaller:

> As Freud observed, the very acts that are forbidden by religion are practiced in the name of religion. In such cases – as, for

instance, murder in the name of religion – religion can also do entirely without miniaturisation. Those adamantly militant advocates of human life, for example, who oppose abortion, will not stop short of actually murdering clinical personnel. Radical right-wing opponents of male homosexuality in the USA act in a similar way. They organise so-called 'gay bashings' in the course of which they beat up and finally rape gays. The ultimate homicidal or homosexual gratification of drives can therefore also be attained, if it only fulfils the condition of evoking the semblance of a counter-measure. What seems to be 'opposition' then has the effect that the X to be fended off can appear itself and be taken for a non-X.[26]

What we encounter here is a textbook case of Hegelian 'oppositional determination': in the figure of the gay basher raping a gay, the gay encounters himself in its oppositional determination, i.e. tautology (self-identity) appears as the highest contradiction. This is the immanent contradiction at the very core of the Church's identity, making it the main anti-Christian force today. Legend says that when, in 1804, the Pope was approaching Napoleon to put the Emperor's crown on his head, Napoleon took the crown from his hands and put it on his head alone; the Pope quipped back: 'I know your aim is to destroy Christianity. But believe me, Sire, you will fail – the Church has been trying to do this for 2000 years and still didn't succeed ...' With people like Cardinal Rode from Slovenia, we can see how the Church continues with its efforts, and there is no reason to rejoice at this sad fact – the Christian legacy is all too precious and, today, more pertinent than ever.

Srećko Horvat

8

IN THE LAND OF BLOOD AND MONEY: ANGELINA JOLIE AND THE BALKANS

When the world's most famous humanitarian philosopher publishes a panegyric on the directorial debut of the world's most famous Hollywood humanitarian actress, one shouldn't be surprised. Writing in *The Huffington Post*, Bernard-Henri Lévy described Angelina Jolie's directorial debut *In the Land of Blood and Honey* (2011), a love story set against the background of the Bosnian War, as 'a film that, to borrow Godard's expression, is not just a film, but a just film, rendering justice to the dead and honour to the survivors ... Consider this Bosnian society that beheld, there, its most painful secret. Here is, suddenly, a great actress, and a great lady as well, who has used her prestige so that, for the first time, they might be allowed to raise their downcast heads.'[27]

In the Land of Blood and Honey, which opened at the Berlin Film Festival in February 2012 and arrived at ex-Yugoslavian cinemas shortly after, has not been met with quite the same degree of enthusiasm from certain quarters. From the outset, the film has generated controversy, including protests by Bosnian women (who are now praising the film), a plagiarism suit, death threats and allegations that Serbian hackers had downgraded the film's Internet ratings.

Once Jolie's tour started, however, the film received huge media attention, at least in Bosnia and Herzegovina and Croatia, with presidents, diplomats and city mayors welcoming the Hollywood star as if she were another Clinton visiting our area again. The only difference is that Clinton never actually visited Zagreb in 1996; he just landed at the airport in his famous leather jacket and had a short conversation with the president. Jolie at least stayed in Zagreb for a few hours, visited the cinema and went straight back to the airport. It was a huge spectacle for a small country like Croatia and, of course, almost no-one talked about the film itself.

The film tells the story of Danijel, a soldier fighting for the Bosnian Serbs, and Ajla, a Bosnian Muslim who was involved with him before the war and is now a captive in the concentration camp he oversees. It's a bad repetition of the same good old story depicted most recently in *The Reader* (Stephen Daldry, 2008), and unforgettably in *The Night Porter* (Liliana Cavani, 1974). In short, it's a story about the perpetrator and the victim and a reversal of these perspectives as the story goes on. On the one hand, you have a war criminal (a concentration camp guard in *The Reader*, the former SS officer in *The Night Porter*, the Serbian officer in Jolie's film), and on the other hand, you have the victim (the boy who read to the concentration camp guard, the concentration camp survivor, the innocent Muslim woman in the Bosnian war). What all three films have in common is a fatal love affair between a criminal and an innocent victim, the only difference being that, in *The Reader*, the boy finds out eight years later, when as a law student, he observes a trial of several women (including his former lover) accused of letting 300 Jewish women die in a burning church.

Common to all these films is that the roles become less and less clear as the story develops. The best example is *The Night*

Porter, where thirteen years after the concentration camp, Lucia meets Maximilian again, who is now working at a Vienna hotel; instead of exposing him, she falls back into their sadomasochistic relationship. The relationship is what Primo Levi – remembering the case of the *Sonderkommando*, the 'special units' of camp inmates in charge of bringing their neighbours to the gas chambers – calls the 'gray zone', the zone in which the 'long chain of conjunction between victim and executioner' comes loose. Or, as Giorgio Agamben puts it in his *Remnants of Auschwitz*, 'where the oppressed becomes oppressor and the executioner in turn appears as victim. A gray, incessant alchemy in which good and evil and, along with them, all the metals of traditional ethics reach their point of fusion.'[28]

The best expression of this new *terra ethica* was articulated by Michael in Bernhard Schlink's novel *The Reader*, on which the film was based: 'I wanted simultaneously to understand Hanna's crime and to condemn it. But it was too terrible for that. When I tried to understand it, I had the feeling I was failing to condemn it as it must be condemned. When I condemned it as it must be condemned, there was no room for understanding. But even as I wanted to understand Hanna, failing to understand her meant betraying her all over again. I could not resolve this. I wanted to pose myself both tasks – understanding and condemnation. But it was impossible to do both.'[29] In other words, when we try to understand the crime, then we stop condemning it; and when we condemn, then we stop understanding it.

So, what is missing in Jolie's film? First, the narrative is shallow and the characters are flat; except for in a few dialogues, we don't see all the horror of the characters' doubts ending in the abyss of the impossibility of distinguishing good and evil. What we have in *In the Land of Blood and*

Honey is exactly the opposite of Nietzsche's famous formula: 'That which is done out of love always takes place beyond good and evil.' The Muslim woman betrays her lover, and her lover, the Serbian officer, kills her. In the film, there is no love that is superior to (ethnic) differences: Ajla chooses her (Muslim) side, and Danijel chooses his (Serbian) side. Instead of withdrawing into an isolated universe like the couple from *The Night Porter*, condemning themselves consciously and readily to a life without Muslims and Serbs, without food or essential supplies, they choose to remain faithful to the constructed difference (Serb/Muslim) against which they have been resisting.

This brings us to the main ideological problem of the film: the film's intention is to blur the standard dichotomy of perpetrator-victim by telling the story of a Muslim woman who falls in love with a Serbian officer, yet it does precisely the opposite. There is no big tragedy: Ajla has no moral doubts like Michael in *The Reader* and is happy in her self-chosen cell, where she can paint and enjoy dinners with her partner; Danijel, meanwhile, is merely serving his father, a Bosnian-Serb general. Here we have a superficial recreation of the old Oedipal Complex, which is again deprived of its tragic dimension. When Danijel's father allows another soldier to rape Ajla, Danijel later kills the soldier; but instead of finally standing up to his father, he continues to serve him, in the end doing exactly what his father would wish him to do: kill his mistress. The only potentially subversive element of the film is the enunciation of the simple, perhaps even naive, word 'sorry'. Instead of trying to find a solution together with his lover (why not the *Night Porter* solution of escaping to a deserted villa in the mountains above Sarajevo?), Danijel merely repeats a castrated 'sorry' (for the raped women in the camp he oversees, etc.); later, after revealing the shelter of

Danijel and his Serbian unit, Ajla repeats the same excuse ('izvini').

Difficult as this is to imagine – surely Danijel would have tried to explain to Alja the reasons for his taking part in ethnic cleansing – this is the point of the film where the story resembles the ancient myth of Echo and Narcissus. Ajla (a Muslim) as Echo who, cursed by the jealous gods, is never allowed to speak for herself (like all the raped women in the camp) and condemned to repeat the ends of others' phrases; and Danijel (a Bosnian Serb) as Narcissus, who can see only his own image and ends up falling into a trap of his own making (aided by his father). There is a memorable part in Kirby Dick and Amy Ziering Kofman's documentary *Derrida* in which Jacques Derrida explains this deadlock: 'In a certain way, she [Echo] appropriates his language. In repeating the language of another, she signs her own love. In repeating, she communicates with him. She speaks her own name by just repeating his words. And as always with speech, one is blind. And at base, Echo blindly but quite lucidly corresponds to Narcissus. It's a story of love, after all. She corresponds to Narcissus who is also blind, because Narcissus realises that he can only see himself, that it's only his own image he is seeing in the water. To see only oneself is a form of blindness. One sees nothing else. Echo and Narcissus then are two blind people who love each other. Now how do two blind people love each other? That's the question.'[30]

In repeating the word 'sorry', Ajla is responding to Danijel in his own words, and in repeating she communicates with him: yes, she loves him, but she betrays him for the same reason that he betrayed her when he was allowing the atrocities, seeking forgiveness with a simple and meaningless 'sorry'. The real subversion – maybe only this could have saved the film – would have been if Danijel had accepted her apology and gone on as if nothing had happened, as Ajla had done previously: 'Yes, I know we are following ideological constructs, that there are no real differences between Muslims and Serbs, and yes, I know that you were only doing your duty and that you wanted to protect your neighbours, but I still love you and I don't care about your betrayal because it's just another fall into the trap of ethnic hatred.'

What is missing in Jolie's film is exactly this tragic dimension of fatal love. The film thus not only misrepresents tragic love itself but also its potential to go one step further. This could be best illustrated by the strange case of Andrej Nikolaidis, the well-known Montenegrin writer. Nikolaidis was born and raised in Sarajevo, but managed to flee in 1992 and settle in Montenegro. A consistent anti-war activist and promoter of human rights, in 2004 Nikolaidis published a piece entitled 'The Executioner's Apprentice'. In it, he denounced the Serbian director Emir Kusturica for having been one of Serbia's biggest media stars at a time 'when Milošević's war propaganda supported people who had some-thing stupid but patriotic to say and created news for people who were insensitive to human suffering, blind to their own guilt, and idiotic enough to believe in their own righteous-ness.'[31] Nikolaidis was successfully sued by the Serbian director for libel; after several appeals he was forced to pay 12,000 Euros in damages to Kusturica for causing 'mental anguish'. In January 2012, Nikolaidis published a new text titled 'What is Left of Greater Serbia'; in it, he dared to offer a completely different explanation of an attempted terrorist attack during the official celebration of the twentieth anniversary of the Republika Srpska, one of the two main political entities of Bosnia and Herzegovina (in)famous for of its 'special ties agreement' with Serbia. What followed was an unprecedented controversy that provoked a series of threats to Nikolaidis and even an official diplomatic dispute between Serbia and Montenegro.

What was the problem? Nikolaidis had cited Walter Benjamin's famous proverb that 'there is no document of civilisation which is not at the same time a document of barbarism', claiming that the political entity of the Republika Srpska was a product of genocide. It would have been 'a civilisational step forward', continued Nikolaidis, had the unsuccessful terrorist used the dynamite not because of national and ethnic hatred, but because 'he was a dissatisfied worker who understood that national and religious antagonism was just a masque under which the elite hides the basic antagonism of every society – class antagonism.'[32] Soon after, a Serbian daily claimed on its front page that Nikolaidis was a terrorist who intended to kill the Serbian president and the Patriarch of the Serbian Orthodox church. Informed by journalists that Nikolaidis had recently received the European Union Prize for Literature, the president of Republika Srpska, Milorad Dodik, answered: 'Feel free to quote me: fuck his literature!' It was only a matter of time before Emir Kusturica would show up: when he did, he didn't resist describing Nikolaidis as a 'Montenegrin Taliban' who 'encourages terrorism in the Balkans'. Last but not least, Kusturica threatened to sue Nikolaidis again! It should be added that Kusturica and his 'No Smoking Orchestra' perform a song called 'Wanted Man', which is dedicated to none other than Radovan Karadžić, the first president of the Republika Srpska currently facing war crimes charges in The Hague.

So, again, what's the problem? The problem is that the disputed paragraph in which Nikolaidis talks about 'a civilisational step forward' is many things, but not nationalism: it opposes any sort of nationalism. The failed terrorist attack would have been 'a civilisational step forward', according to

Nikolaidis, had the poor terrorist realised that it's not about national hatred but about class struggle. And this is exactly the biggest problem of Angelina Jolie's film. Once again we have the same old story about the Serbs and Muslims who couldn't live in one country; the story about war as the result of ethnic hatred and nationalism. At no point in the film is there even a trace of other causes for the fall of Yugoslavia; only old myths about Serbs proud of their role in defending Europe from the Muslims, etc. So when Bernard-Henri Lévy claims that the film is set in a 'blind spot in twentieth century history' he is right – only that the 'blind spot' is not the Bosnian war as such. Srebrenica is not only being used apropos of Syria as justification for 'humanitarian inter-vention', but has been (mis)used for the last two decades all around the world. In other words, isn't Lévy, who called on Sarkozy to demand intervention in Libya, himself obscuring the causes of such interventions? Might we not also pose the question: why Syria and not Israel? Why isn't Lévy praising a film about the Israeli atrocities going on today in the West Bank, instead of a war that happened in the Balkans twenty years ago?

Of course, we still feel the consequences of the war in all regions of ex-Yugoslavia, from Croatia, Bosnia and Herze-govina, to Serbia and Kosovo. And, yes, Jolie's film was a big step in raising awareness about the estimated 50,000 Bosnian Muslim women and girls raped by Serbian forces during the first years of the war.[33] But if we conduct a simple experiment and move the film from Bosnia to any other war zone, removing the occasional references to Serbian ideology, wouldn't the film keep on functioning? That's the problem of *In the Land of Blood and Honey*: the only cause it can find for the conflict is ethnic hatred (and sexual lust). Yet at the time of its Croatian premiere, the minister of finance was announcing new austerity measures and privations, not only in healthcare and social security but also in prisons. The same goes for the rest of the ex-Yugoslavian region, where 'war tycoons' first used the chaos created by the war to rob ('privatise') state companies and industries (there is not a single trace of this 'special unit' in Jolie's film), and later where 'structural adjustments' are being carried out officially and legally by the state.[34]

When one Bosnian film critic said, 'Angelina Jolie's film is the best thing to happen to Bosnia and Herzegovina since the Dayton Agreement', one should reply by saying the opposite: what is finally needed for all ex-Yugoslavian countries is a land not of blood and honey but a *Land of Blood and Money*: a film that would show how the atrocities were carried out not only in the name of the Nation or Ethnic Belonging but – as always – in the name of Money. Those, like Bernard-Henri Lévy, who think the film conveys the 'truth' about the Yugoslavian war are either ignorant or deliberately conceal the real issue; they fall into the same trap as the Serbian soldier who killed his greatest love because, in the end, he started to believe the story told by his vicious father. In the end, what remains is not renewed interest in the war, but only the media spectacle and questions to Jolie such as: 'Will you visit Croatia's beautiful coast next summer?' Her answer: 'Brad is already looking at the photos and is interested.' So much for Lévy's 'blind spot'. As the official slogan of the Croatian Tourist Board puts it: 'Small country for a big holiday.'

Slavoj Žižek

9

THE TURKISH MARCH

The unofficial anthem of the European Union, heard at numerous political, cultural and sporting public events, is the 'Ode an die Freude' melody from the last movement of Beethoven's Ninth Symphony: a true 'empty signifier' that can stand for anything. In France, it was elevated by Romain Rolland into the a humanist ode to the brotherhood of all people ('the Marseillaise of humanity'). In 1938, it was performed as the highpoint of *Reichsmusiktage* and later for Hitler's birthday; in the China of the Cultural Revolution, in the desire to reject European classics, it was redeemed as a piece of progressive class struggle, while in today's Japan, it has achieved cult status, being woven into the very social fabric with its alleged message of 'joy through suffering'. Up until the 1970s, i.e. during the time when both the West and East German Olympic teams had to perform together, as one German team, the anthem played for the German gold medal was the 'Ode to Joy', while, simultaneously, the Rhodesian white supremacist regime of Ian Smith which proclaimed independence in the late 1960s in order to maintain apartheid also proclaimed the same song its national anthem. Even Abimael Guzman, the (now imprisoned) leader of the ultra-terrorist *Sendero Luminoso*, when asked what music he loved, mentioned the forth movement of Beethoven's Ninth. So we can easily imagine a fictional performance at which all sworn enemies, from Hitler to Stalin, from Bush to Saddam, for a moment forget their adversities and participate in the same magic moment of ecstatic brotherhood.

However, before we dismiss the fourth movement as a piece 'destroyed through social usage,' as Adorno put it, let us note some peculiarities of its structure. In the middle of the movement, after we hear the main melody (the Joy theme) in three orchestral and three vocal variations, at the first climax, something unexpected happens which has bothered critics for the last 180 years since the first performance: at bar 331, the tone changes totally, and, instead of the solemn hymnal progression, the same 'Joy' theme is repeated in the *marcia Turca* ('Turkish march') style, borrowed from the military music for wind and percussion instruments that 18th century European armies adopted from the Turkish Janissaries. The mode at that point is that of a carnivalesque popular parade, a mocking spectacle (some critics even compared the grunts of the bassoons and bass drum that accompany the beginning of the *marcia Turca* to farts!). And after this point, everything goes wrong; the simple solemn dignity of the first part of the movement is never recovered: after this 'Turkish' part and in a clear counter-movement to it, the choral-like music (dismissed by some critics as a 'Gregorian fossil') seems to retreat into innermost religiosity and tries to render the ethereal image of millions of people kneeling down, contemplating in awe the distant sky and searching for the loving paternal God who must dwell above the canopy of stars ('ueberm Sternezelt muss ein lieber Vater wohnen'). However, the music then seems to get stuck when the word 'muss,' first rendered by the basses, is repeated by the tenors and altos, and finally by the sopranos; as if this repeated conjuring presents a desperate attempt to convince us (and itself) of what it knows is not true, making the line 'a loving father must dwell' into a desperate act of beseeching, and thus attesting to the fact that there is nothing beyond the canopy of stars, no loving father to protect us and to guarantee our brotherhood. Yet the final cadenza is the strangest of them all, sounding not at all like Beethoven but more like a puffed up version of the finale of Mozart's *Abduction from the Seraglio*, combining the 'Turkish' elements with a fast rococo spectacle. (And let us not forget the lesson of Mozart's opera: the figure of the oriental despot is presented there as a true enlightened Master). The finale is thus a weird mixture of Orientalism and regression into late 18th century classicism, a double retreat from the historical present, a silent admission of the purely fantastical character of the joy of the all-encompassing brotherhood. If there ever was a music that literally 'deconstructs itself,' this is it – no wonder that already in 1826, only two years after the first performance, some reviewers described the finale as 'a festival of hatred towards all that can be called human joy.'

What, then, is the solution? To shift the entire perspective and to render problematic the very first part of the fourth movement: things do not really go wrong only at the bar 331, with the entrance of the *marcia Turca*, they go wrong from the very beginning. One should accept that there is something of an insipid fake in the very core of 'Ode to Joy', so that the chaos that enters after bar 331 is a kind of the 'return of the repressed,' a *symptom* of what was wrong from the very beginning. What if we have overly-domesticated the 'Ode to Joy', what if we got all too used to it as a symbol of joyful brotherhood? What if we should confront it anew, reject it for what is false in it?

Does the same not hold for Europe today? After inviting millions, from the highest to the lowest (worm) to embrace, the second strophe ominously ends: 'But he who cannot rejoice, let him steal weeping away. /*Und wer's nie gekonnt, der stehle weinend sich aus dem Bund.*/' The irony of Beethoven's 'Ode to Joy' being the unofficial European anthem that it is, is that the main cause of today's crisis of the Union is precisely Turkey: according to most of the polls, the main reason behind those who voted NO at the last referendums in France and Netherlands was their opposition to Turkish membership. The NO can be grounded in rightist-populist terms ('no' to the Turkish threat to our culture, 'no' to the cheap Turkish immigrant labour), or in liberal-multiculturalist terms (Turkey should not be allowed in because, in its treatment of the Kurds, it doesn't display enough respect for human rights). And the opposite view, the YES, is as false as Beethoven's final cadenza ... So, should Turkey be allowed into the Union or should it be left to 'steal itself weeping out of the union (*Bund*)'? Can Europe survive the 'Turkish march'?

As in the finale of Beethoven's Ninth, what if the true problem is not Turkey, but the basic melody itself, the song of European unity as it is played to us by the post-political pragmatic-technocratic elite of Brussels? What we need is a totally new main melody, a new definition of Europe itself. The problem of Turkey, the perplexity of the European Union with regard to what to do with Turkey, is not about Turkey as such, but the confusion about what Europe itself is.

Where, then, are we today? Europe lies in the great pincers between America on the one side and China on the other. America and China, seen metaphysically, are both the same: the same hopeless frenzy of unchained technology and of the rootless organisation of the average person. When the farthest corner of the globe has been conquered technically and can be exploited economically; when any incident you like, in any place you like, at any time you like, becomes accessible as fast as you like; when, through TV 'live coverage,' you can simultaneously 'experience' a battle in the Iraqi desert and an opera performance in Beijing; when, in a global digital network, time is nothing but speed, instantaneity, and simultaneity; when a winner in a reality TV-show counts as a great hero of a people; then, yes, there still looms like a spectre over all this uproar the question: what for? – where to? – and what then?

Everybody who is minimally acquainted with Heidegger will, of course, easily recognise in this paragraph an ironic paraphrase of Heidegger's diagnosis of the situation in Europe from the mid 1930s (*Einfuehrung in die Metaphysik*). There effectively is a need, among us Europeans, for what Heidegger called *Auseinandersetzung* (interpretive confrontation) with others as well as with Europe's own past in all its scope, from its Ancient and Judeo-Christian roots to the recently deceased idea of the Welfare-State. Europe is today split between the so-called Anglo-Saxon model, which asks for acceptance of 'modernisation' (adaptation to the rules of the new global order) – and the French-German model – which asks us to save as much as possible of the 'old European' welfare-state. Although opposed, these two options are two sides of the same coin, and our true path is neither to return to any idealised form of the past – these models are clearly exhausted – nor to convince Europeans that, if we are to survive as a world power, we should accommodate ourselves to the recent trends of globalisation as fast as possible. Nor can the task be seen as what is arguably the worst option: the search for a 'creative synthesis' between European traditions of globalisation, with the aim being to achieve something one is tempted to call 'globalisation with a European face.'

Every crisis is in itself an instigation for a new beginning; every collapse of short-term strategic and pragmatic measures (for financial reorganisation of the Union, etc.) a blessing in disguise, an opportunity to rethink the very foundations. What we need is a retrieval-through-repetition (*Wieder-Holung*): through a critical confrontation with the entire European tradition, one should repeat the question 'What is Europe?' or rather, 'What does it mean for us to be Europeans?', and thus formulate a new inception.

The task is difficult; it compels us to take the great risk of stepping into the unknown – yet its only alternative is slow decay, the gradual transformation of Europe into what Greece was for the mature Roman Empire, a destination for nostalgic cultural tourism with no effective relevance.

In his *Notes Towards a Definition of Culture*, the great conservative T.S.Eliot remarked that there are moments when the only choice is the one between sectarianism and non-belief, when the only way to keep a religion alive is to perform a sectarian split from its main corpse. This is our only chance today: only by means of a 'sectarian split' from the standard European legacy, by cutting ourselves off the decaying corpse of the old Europe, can we keep the renewed European legacy alive.

SREĆKO HORVAT

10

WAR AND PEACE IN EUROPE: 'BEI DEN SORGLOSEN'

Non vi si pensa, quanto sangue costa
(No-one thinks how much blood it will cost)
Dante, Paradiso XXIX

'Mr Godot told me to tell you that he won't come this evening, but surely tomorrow,' a boy said in Serbo-Croatian with a voice heavy with embarrassment and regret. In the theatre, as the New York Times reports, 'The only sounds were from the street outside, of a United Nations armoured vehicle thundering past on its steel tracks, and, from somewhere in the distance, the blast of a mortar shell.' It was the year 1993. 'The audience sat stock still. Among them were surgeons from the city's main hospital, soldiers from the front, Government officials who must juggle allotments of food for a population in growing hunger, people who have lost fathers and sisters and sons, and one man in a wheelchair, an actor before the war, who lost both legs when a mortar struck outside his home last summer.' It was Sarajevo. When Susan Sontag decided to stage a production of *Waiting for Godot*, it was a clear message to Europe: just one or two hours from the main European airports in Rome, Vienna, Berlin and Paris, a city was bleeding to death. If *Waiting for Godot* was a play that achieved the almost impossible, a play in which nothing happens twice, then the siege of Sarajevo, the longest siege of a capital city in the history of modern warfare, was further proof that in Europe nothing happens all the time. It wasn't for the first time that only a few hours away from the tragedy of some people, other people, in European capitals, were living calmly, comfortable and not even trying to think about what was happening out of their comfort zone.

It is the year 2013. Hundreds of thousands of people are gathered to hear Obama's inaugural speech. Everyone is full of excitement; they believe it's a historical moment. And then Obama says: 'We, the people, still believe that enduring security and lasting peace do not require perpetual war ... We will show the courage to try and resolve our differences with other nations peacefully – not because we are naïve about the dangers we face, but because engagement can more durably lift suspicion and fear ... And we must be a source of hope to the poor, the sick, the marginalised, the victims of prejudice – not out of mere charity, but because peace in our time requires the constant advance of those principles that our common creed describes: tolerance and opportunity; human dignity and justice.' At the same time, when the Nobel Peace Laureate president gives his talk and the people 'showed the courage to try and resolve differences with other nations peacefully', the US drone aircraft was bombing Yemen and Pakistan, Afghanistan and Somalia. Here is a list, compiled by the organisation *DronesWatch*, of children killed by US drones in Pakistan:

Noor Aziz [8]
Abdul Wasit [17]
Noor Syed [8]

Wajid Noor [9]
Syed Wali Shah [7]
Ayeesha [3]
Qari Alamzeb [14]
Shoaib [8]
Hayatullah KhaMohammad [16]
Tariq Aziz [16]
Sanaullah Jan [17]
Maezol Khan [8]
Nasir Khan [?]
Naeem Khan [?]
Naeemullah [?]
Mohammad Tahir [16]
Azizul Wahab [15]
Fazal Wahab [16]
Ziauddin [16]
Mohammad Yunus [16]
Fazal Hakim [19]
Ilyas [13]
Sohail [7]
Asadullah [9]
khalilullah [9]
Noor Mohammad [8]
Khalid [12]
Saifullah [9]
Mashooq Jan [15]
Nawab [17]
Sultanat Khan [16]
Ziaur Rahman [13]
Noor Mohammad [15]
Mohammad Yaas Khan [16]
Qari Alamzeb [14]
Ziaur Rahman [17]

Abdullah [18]
Ikramullah Zada [17]
Inayatur Rehman [16]
Shahbuddin [15]
Yahya Khan [16]
Rahatullah |17]
Mohammad Salim [11]
Shahjehan [15]
Gul Sher Khan [15]
Bakht Muneer [14]
Numair [14]
Mashooq Khan [16]
Ihsanullah [16]
Luqman [12]
Jannatullah [13]
Ismail [12]
Taseel Khan [18]
Zaheeruddin [16]
Qari Ishaq [19]
Jamshed Khan [14]
Alam Nabi [11]
Qari Abdul Karim [19]
Rahmatullah [14]
Abdus Samad [17]
Siraj [16]
Saeedullah [17]
Abdul Waris [16]
Darvesh [13]
Ameer Said [15]
Shaukat [14]
Inayatur Rahman [17]
Salman [12]
Fazal Wahab [18]

Baacha Rahman [13]
Wali-ur-Rahman [17]
Iftikhar [17]
Inayatullah [15]
Mashooq Khan [16]
Ihsanullah [16]
Luqman [12]
Jannatullah [13]
Ismail [12]
Abdul Waris [16]
Darvesh [13]
Ameer Said [15]
Shaukat [14]
Inayatur Rahman [17]
Adnan [16]
Najibullah [13]
Naeemullah [17]
Hizbullah [10]
Kitab Gul [12]
Wilayat Khan [11]
Zabihullah [16]
Shehzad Gul [11]
Shabir [15]
Qari Sharifullah [17]
Shafiullah [16]
Nimatullah [14]
Shakirullah [16]
Talha [8]

There is another list, which I witnessed after the Arab Spring in summer 2012. It was in Tunisia, in a small fishing village called Ksibet el Mediouni. Once the Almoravids had their forts here in order to fight against Christian intrusions in this part of the Tunisian coast. Today, many immigrants, looking for a better life, decide to sail on the waves of the Mediterranean Sea to the 'Fortress Europe' from this very shore. Many of them drown on their way, and those who succeed to escape from their misfortune often inhabit the *banlieues* in Paris or suburbs in Rome, selling souvenirs, working in restaurants or cleaning toilets, with the constant threat of deportation. To warn of a rapidly growing problem, in early July 2012 an initiative called 'Boats 4 People' sent a ship from Palermo to Tunisia, with activists from Italy, Germany, France, Niger, Mali and Tunisia who had decided to repeat that route often passed by immigrants. As a result of the conflict in Libya, almost one million people sought refuge in Tunisia, Egypt, Chad and Niger, while the European Union – which supposedly just fought for human rights in Libya and now in Mali – adopted a repressive approach, through the border control agency Frontex, often leaving the poor refugees to drown. The war in Libya is supposedly over, but the war against immigrants continues. In 2012 alone, more than 1,000 immigrants died in the Mediterranean Sea.

There at the shore of Ksibet el Mediouni we were waiting for the boats to arrive. More than 200 people gathered, including widows whose husbands or children never returned from the mythical Europe. At one point, a big list is stretched across the pier. A list of 16,175 documented deaths because of the 'Fortress Europe' from 1 January 1993 to 30 May 2012, with the exact date of death, name, country of origin and manner of death. Most of them, however, don't even have names: NN from Afghanistan drowned after smugglers threw him from the boat just off the coast of Calabria; Alain Hatungimana (one of the few whose name is known) from Burundi committed suicide in the Netherlands, because she feared that she could be deported with her two children; an immigrant from Egypt died from hypothermia; a boy from Afghanistan suffocated in a truck in which he had hid to avoid border control; refugees from Macedonia drowned in the Rhine while trying to swim across the border between Austria and Switzerland; Nazmieh Charour, a 20-year-old Palestinian, committed suicide in prison in Berlin having been told she would be deported; a Kurdistan man was shot in front of a refugee camp in Dülmen. During the 1990s, the list also includes many from Bosnia, Croatia, Serbia, and lately, the country of origin is often Kosovo.

We can, for sure, find similar lists like this all over the world today. But to understand how it is possible that some people leave undisturbed while others are dying, we have to turn to an author who witnessed two World Wars but didn't survive the second because he decided to take his own life. It is, of course, the Austrian writer Stefan Zweig. In his autobiography *The World of Yesterday* (*Die Welt von Gestern*) not only did he cover the biggest historical events of the first part of the twentieth century, he described in detail how it was possible for Hitler to come to power. Just a few days before the eruption of the First World War, he discovered something strange. It was summer 1914, which was '*sommerlicher*' ('more summery') than any summer before, says Zweig, and he describes the atmosphere. He was having a holiday in Baden, near Vienna, a small romantic city that was once Beethoven's favourite *Sommeraufenthalt*. 'In light summer dresses, gay and carefree, the crowds moved about to the music in the park. The day was mild; a cloudless sky lay over the broad chestnut trees; it was a day made to be happy in. The vacation days would soon set in for the adults and children, and on this holiday they antici-pated the entire summer, with its fresh air, its lush green, and the forgetting of all daily cares.'

Of course we can pose the question how could anyone have

known the Bosnian Serb student Gavrilo Princip would shoot Franz Ferdinand in Sarajevo and the First World War would break out. But what Zweig described so well in June 1914 repeated itself at the end of the war again. The best depiction of this 'carefreeness' wasn't developed in Zweig's auto-biography, but in an article which appeared under the title 'A Carefree Life' in *The New Free Press* in 1918.[35] It is a story about a visit to the *Sorglosen* (care-free people) in the Alps of St. Moritz, who live a luxurious life with fresh air, they laugh and ski, they play polo and hockey, and they dance. At the same time, 'Europe falls into rubble. The gypsy band fiddles away. Ten thousand people die every day. Dinner is over and the masked ball begins. Widows sit shivering in all the chambers of the world. A bare-shouldered marquise steps forward, a masked Chinese opposite. Masks and more masks pour in. And truly, they are real – not a human face amongst them. The mirror sconces are lit. The dance commences; sweet, soft rhythms, while elsewhere ships sink into the deep and trenches are stormed.'[36]

So what we have here are not only people who enjoy the summer because they still don't know the assassination in Sarajevo would happen, these are people who know very well what they are doing, but they are doing it anyhow (this is the old formula of fetishist disavowal by Octave Mannoni: *Je sais bien, mais quand meme* ...). After the First World War, Zweig was convinced such atrocities could never happen again. But the same pattern of 'carefreeness' would repeat itself again. Just before the Second World War, Zweig noticed: 'My house in Salzburg lay so close to the border that with the naked eye I could view the Berchtesgaden mountain on which Adolf Hitler's house stood, an uninviting and very disturbing neighbourhood. This proximity to the German border, however, gave me an opportunity to judge the threat to the

Austrian situation better than my friends in Vienna. In that city the café observers and even men in the Government regarded National Socialism as something that was happening "over there" and that could in no way affect Austria.'[37] Doesn't this remind us of Sarajevo as well? Moreover, the biggest paradox doesn't lie in the fact that we don't know what is happening in a neighbour country, but sometimes we don't even know what is happening in our own country. A similar event occurred during the civil war in Croatia as well. Recently, a Croatian TV documentary showed a testimony by a war reporter who remembers the summer, which was maybe also *sommerlicher* than any summer before: people in Slavonia were having fun and swimming at baths, while he was returning from Vukovar where the war was already going on. On the one hand, you have people who are still not aware what is happening, or they know something, but can't believe in it. On the other hand, you have someone who is just returning from the horrors of a bloodbath and can't believe they can't believe. It is as if parallel worlds are living in close proximity, not knowing the other world exists, but with these small interruptions of the Real.

In an interview for the *New York Times Book Review*, published in July 1940, just two years before his suicide, Zweig, the author of the unforgettable love story from the *Brief einer Unbekannten (Letter from an Unknown Woman)*, connects this problem of parallel worlds with the (im)possibility of literature: 'How can the old themes still command our attention? A man and a woman meet, fall in love, have an affair – that sort of thing was once a story. One day it will be a story again. But how can we bear to live amidst such triviality with a clear conscience now?'[38] He was writing about the tragedies of the Second World War, but couldn't the following words be applied to the 16,175 dead immigrants in the Mediterranean as well? 'On every ship, in every travel agency and at every consulate you can hear the tales of insignificant, anonymous people about adventures and odysseys that are no less dangerous and exciting than those of Ulysses. If someone, without altering a single word, were to print the documents of these refugees ... it would yield hundreds of volumes of stories, each and every one of them more gripping and amazing than those of Jack London and Maupassant.'[39] As we can see, what bothers Zweig is not only the fact that 'normal life' continues in the capitals not touched by the war, but it is the same old doubt – expressed almost a decade later by Adorno ('To write poetry after Auschwitz is barbaric') – how can we still write fiction having all these destinies in front of us? Zweig goes even so far as to risk the hypothesis that all literature in the following years would have only a documentary character. We can't know whether Zweig would have changed his mind, if he had survived, but already in his *Negative Dialectics*, Adorno offered a revision of his own famous dictum, saying that 'Perennial suffering has as much right to expression as a tortured man has to scream.'

It is exactly Salzburg, the city where Zweig lived from 1919 to 1933 at the Kapuzinerberg until he was forced to flee to London, in which another tragic figure of the twentieth century took his own life. In 1978 Jean Améry committed suicide in the Salzburg Hotel, Östereichischer Hof. It is a tragic irony that today the hotel is named 'Hotel Sacher': on the one hand, you have the 'homo sacer', in Agamben's definition not only the traditional figure of Roman law who can be killed without the killer being regarded as a murderer but also the best description of the Jews in the Holocaust – Améry who survived Auschwitz, Buchenwald and Bergen-Belsen. On the other hand, you have the 'homo sacher', the inhabitants of the famous hotel who don't even know what a heavy burden their fellow man carries all his life. And are not all of us the walking proof of such 'homo sacher' who, undisturbed, enjoy today's Europe without borders and without war, although borders and wars exist simultaneously not only in faraway places, in Pakistan or Mali, in the Mediterranean Sea or in refugee camps, but on the corners of our capitals? Are we not being 'carefree' when we speak about the united Europe, although a (political, social and economic) war is happening every day, from the immigrants drowning on our shores or surviving in the suburbs of our cities, to the peripheral countries like Greece or Portugal, where more than 50 per cent of young people don't have a job, from the European troops in Libya and Mali, to the divided island of Cyprus?

And, inevitably, here we come to a recent book written by Robert Menasse under the title *Der Europäische Landbote*.[40] The Austrian writer went to Brussels to write a novel about the capital of the European Union, but instead of literature or fiction he returned with a manifest about a transnational democratic Europe. Here is the opening passage of the book: 'If you take a black pen and draw on a map of Europe all the political borders there have been in the course of written history, in the end the continent is covered by such a dense black web that it almost resembles a uniform black surface. Which black line on this black surface can logically be considered a natural border? If you then take a red pen and draw a line on this map linking the belligerents and marking the battlefields and front lines of every war that ever took place in Europe, the web of borders disappears completely beneath a field of red.'[40]

In short, what we have here is the typical elaboration of Europe's legacy: it is a project mainly aimed at preserving peace. And Menasse shares the positions of Habermas: what is needed is a transnational democratic Europe. The only problem is that neither of them see the connection between the current economical path of the EU and its consequences. To detect the real problem, what we should do is to transform Menasse's passage into the following: if we use a black pen and on a map of Europe draw all the austerity measures, shock-therapies and structural adjustments that have been made in the course of the last twenty years, since the fall of the Berlin Wall, what we will get in the end is a continent with such a black surface that it's almost completely black. Which black line on this black surface can be considered as a natural measure? When we use a red pen and draw all lost jobs, human degradation and protests that have taken place in Europe only in the last couple of years, then the network of austerity measures completely disappears under the red-coloured surface.

What does it mean? The answer is simple, and we have tried to show it in all our arguments in this book: it is precisely the neoliberal path of the EU, with austerity measures and structural adjustments, which is leading to a permanent civil war, not only outside of the European borders where 'our' soldiers are fighting for 'more democracy', but also inside of the European Union, from Greece and Spain, to Slovenia and Croatia. *Non vi si pensa ...*

Slavoj Žižek

II
SAVE US FROM THE SAVIOURS:
EUROPE AND THE GREEKS

Imagine a scene from a dystopian movie that depicts our society in the near future. Uniformed guards patrol half-empty downtown streets at night, on the prowl for immigrants, criminals and vagrants. Those they find are brutalised. What seems like a fanciful Hollywood image is a reality in today's Greece. At night, black-shirted vigilantes from the Holocaust-denying neo-fascist Golden Dawn movement – which won 7 per cent of the vote in the last round of elections, and had the support, it's said, of 50 per cent of the Athenian police – have been patrolling the street and beating up all the immigrants they can find: Afghans, Pakistanis, Algerians. So this is how Europe is defended in the spring of 2012.

The trouble with defending European civilisation against the immigrant threat is that the ferocity of the defence is more of a threat to 'civilisation' than any number of Muslims. With friendly defenders like this, Europe needs no enemies. A hundred years ago, G.K. Chesterton articulated the deadlock in which critics of religion find themselves: 'Men who begin to fight the Church for the sake of freedom and humanity end by flinging away freedom and humanity if only they may fight the Church ... The secularists have not wrecked divine things; but the secularists have wrecked secular things, if that is any comfort to them.' Many liberal warriors are so eager to fight anti-democratic fundamentalism that they end up dispensing with freedom and democracy if only they may fight terror. If the 'terrorists' are ready to wreck this world for love of another, our warriors against terror are ready to wreck democracy out of hatred for the Muslim other. Some of them love human dignity so much that they are ready to legalise torture to defend it. It's an inversion of the process by which fanatical defenders of religion start out by attacking contemporary secular culture and end up sacrificing their own religious credentials in their eagerness to eradicate the aspects of secularism they hate.

But Greece's anti-immigrant defenders aren't the principal danger: they are just a by-product of the true threat, the politics of austerity that have caused Greece's predicament. The next round of Greek elections will be held on 17 June 2012. The European establishment warns us that these elections are crucial: not only the fate of Greece, but maybe the fate of the whole of Europe is in the balance. One outcome – the right one, they argue – would allow the painful but necessary process of recovery through austerity to continue. The alternative – if the 'extreme leftist' SYRIZA party wins – would be a vote for chaos, the end of the (European) world as we know it.

The prophets of doom are right, but not in the way they intend. Critics of our current democratic arrangements complain that elections don't offer a true choice: what we get instead is the choice between a centre-right and a centre-left party whose programmes are almost indistinguishable. On 17 June 2012, there will be a real choice: the establishment (New Democracy and Pasok) on one side, SYRIZA on the other.

And, as is usually the case when a real choice is on offer, the establishment is in a panic: chaos, poverty and violence will follow, they say, if the wrong choice is made. The mere possibility of a SYRIZA victory is said to have sent ripples of fear through global markets. Ideological prosopopoeia has its day: markets talk as if they were persons, expressing their 'worry' at what will happen if the elections fail to produce a government with a mandate to persist with the EU-IMF programme of fiscal austerity and structural reform. The citizens of Greece have no time to worry about these prospects: they have enough to worry about in their everyday lives, which are becoming miserable to a degree unseen in Europe for decades.

Such predictions are self-fulfilling, causing panic and thus bringing about the very eventualities they warn against. If SYRIZA wins, the European establishment will hope that we learn the hard way what happens when an attempt is made to interrupt the vicious cycle of mutual complicity between Brussels' technocracy and anti-immigrant populism. This is why Alexis Tsipras, Syriza's leader, made clear in a recent interview that his first priority, should SYRIZA win, will be to counteract panic: 'People will conquer fear. They will not succumb; they will not be blackmailed.' SYRIZA have an almost impossible task. Theirs is not the voice of extreme left 'madness', but of reason speaking out against the madness of market ideology. In their readiness to take over, they have banished the Left's fear of taking power; they have the courage to clear up the mess created by others. They will need to exercise a formidable combination of principle and pragmatism, of democratic commitment and a readiness to act quickly and decisively where needed. If they are to have even a minimal chance of success, they will need an all-European display of solidarity: not only decent treatment on the part of every other European country, but also more creative ideas, like the promotion of solidarity tourism this summer.

In his *Notes towards the Definition of Culture*, T.S. Eliot remarked that there are moments when the only choice is between heresy and non-belief – i.e., when the only way to keep a religion alive is to perform a sectarian split. This is the position in Europe today. Only a new 'heresy' – represented at this moment by SYRIZA – can save what is worth saving of the European legacy: democracy, trust in people, egalitarian solidarity etc. The Europe we will end up with if SYRIZA is outmanoeuvred is a 'Europe with Asian values' – which, of course, has nothing to do with Asia, but everything to do with the tendency of contemporary capitalism to suspend democracy.

Here is the paradox that sustains the 'free vote' in democratic societies: one is free to choose on condition that one makes the right choice. This is why, when the wrong choice is made (as it was when Ireland rejected the EU constitution), the choice is treated as a mistake, and the establishment immediately demands that the 'democratic' process be repeated in order that the mistake may be corrected. When George Papandreou, then Greek prime minister, proposed a referendum on the Eurozone bailout deal at the end of last year, the referendum itself was rejected as a false choice.

There are two main stories about the Greek crisis in the media: the German-European story (the Greeks are irresponsible, lazy, free-spending, tax-dodging etc, and have to be brought under control and taught financial discipline) and the Greek story (our national sovereignty is threatened by the neoliberal technocracy imposed by Brussels). When it became impossible to ignore the plight of the Greek people, a third story emerged: the Greeks are now presented as humanitarian victims in need of help, as if a war or natural catastrophe had hit the country. While all three stories are false, the third is arguably the most disgusting. The Greeks are not passive victims: they are at war with the European economic establishment, and what they need is solidarity in their struggle, because it is our struggle too.

Greece is not an exception. It is one of the main testing grounds for a new socio-economic model of potentially unlimited application: a depoliticised technocracy in which bankers and other experts are allowed to demolish democracy. By saving Greece from its so-called saviours, we also save Europe itself.

Srećko Horvat

12
'I'M NOT RACIST, BUT ... THE BLACKS ARE COMING!'

In early February 2013, the Croatian daily newspaper, *Jutarnji list*, once again proved itself to a top purveyor of national inflammatory journalism. Following the asylum centre case, being fought in Dugave (a suburb of Zagreb) the reporters published their exclusive 'research' under the headline: 'We're not racists, but the situation is uncomfortable. These people wander around aimlessly and stare at our girls.' The issue started when the local hotel, until recently owned by Croatian Railways, was given over to the Ministry of the Interior and turned into an asylum centre. These 'problems' can best be described by the local residents themselves; one of them says: 'If I knew that one day they would move a haven for asylum seekers here, I'd buy an apartment elsewhere ... I'm not racist, but I get uneasy when I see groups of black men aimlessly wandering around the neighbourhood and watching our children.'[41]

Another resident added, 'It was very nice here until recently. No one warned us that the hotel would be turned into a 'refugee afro-community'. Then suddenly these people of all races and customs started showing up. As I said before, I don't judge people by the colour of their skin, but when someone comes directly from Africa to a European capital, he kind of stands out a little, you know. They are dressed in traditional African clothes, speak an incomprehensible language, roam our streets, often after midnight and shouting to each other as if they were out in the bush. There's this one that constantly yelling; his voice is like a foghorn – horrible! And then we learned that the Porin Hotel was recently established as a new reception centre for asylum seekers.' A third source explained the essence of the problem: 'This summer, these tall black men came and stole our fruit from the trees. Of course, there are decent ones too, that ask nicely. But then in the middle of the night we hear the crashing of branches and came to find them jumping over the garden fence. Some of these black guys are two meters tall.' He added that he was 'not a racist' and that he has always wanted to travel Africa, which he considers the cradle of civilisation.

What is common to all of these statements? In each of them we can identify the form of fetishist denial that the French psychoanalyst Octave Mannoni described in the formula *'Je sais bien, mais quand même.'*[42] As we know, fetishism is defined as the projection of desires and fantasies onto another object or body part (e.g. a fetish for shoes), in order to avoid the subject's confrontation with the castration complex. Even Freud argued that the fetishist is able at one and the same time to believe in his fantasy and to recognise that it is nothing but a fantasy. The problem is, however, that this recognition of the fantasy in no way reduces the power it has over the individual. Mannoni gives two practical examples that explain this very well. The first is from Freud's psycho-analytic practice and the other from his own. Freud once had a patient who was told by a fortune-teller that his son-in-law would die of poisoning that summer. After the summer passed, the patient was taken on by Freud, and admitted, 'I know very well that my son-in-law did not die, but still, the prophecy was so enjoyable.' Another example can be seen in this incident: a telephone call that was for Mannoni was taken by somebody else who mixed up the name of the caller with the name of a poet friend whose visit Mannoni was expecting. Mannoni requested the person who answered the phone to ask the poet friend to come as soon as possible and so that they could have time for a drink before dinner. However, the person who rang the doorbell later was not the poet but a patient. After a brief silence, the satisfied patient admitted, 'Yes, I knew very well that you were joking about a drink before dinner, but still, I was very pleased,' and in the same breath he added, 'especially since my wife thought you were being serious.' Mannoni has immediately connected this with an example from Freud's short text on telepathy: what the shaman guessed rightly was the patient's unconscious, or, in this case, conscious desire. In this case the patient realised the mistake and gave up the fantasy that the psychoanalyst really called him for a drink before dinner, but his wife had made it easy for him, since she enabled him to live the fantasy through her. In one way, the patient has indeed been invited, at least in the eyes of his wife, even though he 'knew very well' that this was not the case.

And thus we return to the tenants of Dugave. Although none of them thought of themselves as a racist, their use of the structure of fetishist denial ('I know very well, but ...') clearly shows that they are. As Freud's patient in some way experienced the desired death of his son-in-law through the mistaken prediction, and just as Mannoni's patient recognised the mistaken phone call but still enjoyed his wife's belief that it was real, so our racists from New Zagreb, in denying their racism, prove that their racism is still alive. The statement 'I am not racist, but ... black people roam the streets, stare at our children, steal our fruit, dress strangely, etc.' reveals that they – whether they qualify as racists or not – are clearly bothered by the 'strange' people and their 'strange' habits. To really prove racism, we can use a single thought experiment. Let us assume that these statements were made about 'regular' residents of Dugave and apply the same ideas to them; 'They roam the streets, steal our fruit, are very tall, etc.' In other words, isn't what these 'black people' do just the same as what the average Croat does? (Although, of course, Croats do not steal). Or let us take another inversion that I owe to one particular asylum seeker, originally from Nigeria, a resident of the afore-mentioned asylum centre. Commenting on the 'report' from the daily newspaper and comments from local residents, he recalled his own experience of visits to schools to help educate the children about asylum seekers and other cultures. Apparently, it was very common for the children in elementary schools come up to him and touch his skin and hair, simply out of naivety and curiosity, because they had never seen a black African before. He also added that the same thing happened in Dugave: if immigrants had been staring at 'our girls' it was because there are no blondes in Nigeria or Afghanistan, and it was as simple as that. The fact that they 'roam the streets' can be explained by the fact that none of them are able to get a job in Croatia (thereby invalidating another myth: 'They will steal our jobs ...') and the fact that they only socialise among themselves can be explained by the sad truth that none of them have been given the Croatian language lessons to which they are entitled by law and which would enable them to integrate with local Croats.

This last episode explains exactly why such 'stories' and fabricated scandals encourage even more hatred and racism. If there is no contact with the Other, the possibility of understanding and learning is greatly reduced. Likewise, if the Croatian Interior Ministry, from 1997 to mid-2011, received about 2,000 applications for asylum and granted asylum to just 42 people, it's no wonder that the residents of Dugave will never know who these are asylum seekers are, and whether they come from Afghanistan, Pakistan or Palestine, not for fun or a desire to 'roam the streets' and 'stare at our girls,' but to escape places that are affected by the war and where life is unsustainable. In 2012, 1193 people applied for asylum in Croatia alone, which is already 50 percent more than the year before. The largest increase is in seekers coming from Somalia; another country that has for almost two decades been hit by a bloody civil war, and a place that can boast of being 'the most dangerous country in the world.' With Croatia joining the European Union, such statistics will only exacerbate and, unfortunately, we can expect not only more cases of fetishist denial of racism, but also the kind of open racism recently expressed by MEP Ruža Tomašić, who said that foreigners have no business in Croatia. Previously, there were the Serbs, and now there are the blacks. The present situation with the *Golden Dawn* in Greece is no longer a distant future, but a present that is just waiting to be mobilised through growing political engagement and actual violence against immigrants.

Before the 'report' published by *Jutarnji list*, the company *Fade In* made an educational documentary called 'Being Different. Identity, prejudice and violence,' back in 2012.[43] Here we can hear not only the usual racist prejudices, but also worrying signs of open racism. During interviews with the residents of Dugave – mothers, fathers, high school pupils and even a Grandma – about their 'immigrant neighbours' the following statements appeared: 'the Blacks', 'sun-baked', 'they wear flip flops in the winter,' 'they aren't people like us', 'they come here only for our beautiful girls, beg for money and steal', 'I don't know why they came here, probably to get a job, and they will get one before you or I do', 'gently deport them back where they came from', 'I have no idea of where they put them, Jasenovac (WWII concentration camp) is not working, so I do not know where they take them' and so on. Here we are no longer dealing with fetishist denial ('I'm not racist, but ...'), but with openly racist messages that include not only outrage against the Other, but also contain a 'proposal' to resolve the situation with deportation and concentration camps.

Another bizarre event, this time from Italy, can reveal just how 'different' immigrants are indeed from us, the so-called 'indigenous' culture. In February 2009, Silvio Berlusconi's government decided to support the campaign against 'un-Italian' meals in Italy, which is trying to persuade Italians to choose more local cuisine. The whole campaign started in Lucca, where the city government went so far as to prohibit the opening of stores selling 'foreign' food within the walls of the old city. Almost simultaneously, the city of Milan brought in a similar law, in order to 'preserve local specialties from the increasing influence of ethnic cuisines.' Of course, this 'culinary racism' – like every form of racism – overlooks the fact that the term 'authentic Italian cuisine' is extremely problematic. Most Italian cuisine, as explained by renowned chef Vittorio Castellani, is actually imported. Tomato sauce is a gift from Peru in the 18th century, and even spaghetti is believed to have been brought from China during the journeys of Marco Polo. Yet, despite these contradictions, 'culinary racism' is not some excessive anomaly, but should be seen as an integral part of the general trend towards xenophobia and the continuing discrimination against immigrants. This campaign is already a powerful blow to the standard of many immigrants who earn their living by selling 'their' food, which has become very popular because of its low cost (in Milan alone, there are nearly 700 ethnic restaurants).

The campaign against non-Italian food, as well as a growing animosity toward immigrants as reflected in the increased policing on the streets or civilian night patrols in Trieste, have their origins in the so-called 'Bossi-Fini' law, of 2002. The principle of that policy is that entry visas must be connected with an employment contract, and that termination of the contract of employment also terminates the visa validity. The 'Bossi-Fini' law paved the way for today's police state that has reduced immigration to mostly seasonal migration. The Bossi-Fini law discussion on migration reminds us of the similar terminology of the restrictive laws on mobility introduced under fascism in 1939, which are exploited by the big Italian industrialists. The point is that employers now literally can blackmail many immigrants, since it depends on them whether their visas be extended or not. An additional problem with the Bossi-Fini law that it is at its core is based on one inherent contradiction, which is based on the relationship between legality and contract in a perfidious Catch 22 situation: on the one hand, the immigrant cannot get a contract if s/he has no legal status, on the other hand, the immigrant may not have legal status if there is no contract. In this context, it is no wonder that in Italy there are only 8,000 immigrants, compared to 40,000-50,000 in France and Germany, respectively. Yet the Berlusconi administration continuously (by sending the army into the streets, initiating night patrols, banning ethic food outlets) created panic – using what Arjun Appadurai calls 'the fear of small numbers'. In this way, they seek to assure that 'the Italian way' is threatened (immigrants are the ones who rape our women, immigrants are the ones who are destroying 'authentic' Italian food, who are stealing our jobs, etc.).

In parallel with the 'politics of fear' are the increasing

policing powers of the state and what Etienne Balibar calls 'institutional racism'.[44] But perhaps 'racism' is too strong a word? Balibar argues that racism has a history of three forms: anti-Semitism, colonialism and racism against blacks in the United States. There is 'internal racism' (directed towards a minority or majority in some cases, such as in South Africa) and 'external racism' (directed towards colonised peoples). However, Balibar does not consider racism the same as nationalism, since the construction of 'race' transcends the boundaries of nation states. Racism is in this sense a kind universalism: based on the universal nature of the human species in the sense that 'foreigners' (immigrants) are not really people – they can drown in the sea, and if one of 'our people' try to save them, then they will be punished.

This is exactly what happens in Italy all the time. In the summer of 2009, a boat with 80 immigrants floated apparently unnoticed in the area between Lampedusa and Libya for almost 20 days. The Italian border police rescued five African immigrants, while the other 75 passengers died after they ran out of food and water. A certain Laura Boldrini from UNHCR, stated that 'every ship that passed these men, and did not help them, violated international maritime law.' However, the catch is that every captain who might have saved the immigrants would have found himself in a dilemma: by not saving them, they violate maritime law (not to mention their own moral integrity), whereas if they saved them, then comes the issue at the port at which they dock with illegal immigrants. In September 2007, seven Tunisian fishermen ended up in court in Sicily because they rescued 44 African migrants who would have otherwise drowned. They were threatened with a prison sentence of up to 15 years for 'aiding illegal immigrants.' One night, the fishermen dropped anchor about 30 miles from the island of Lampedusa and went to sleep, only later to be woken by the screams from a small boat full of starving people, among whom were women and children. The captain decided to take them to the nearest port in Lampedusa, where the whole crew was then arrested. In contrast, some other fishermen who were in a similar situation apparently pushed the immigrants away with sticks, letting them drown. Here, then, we get a true picture of the present situation: those that help people facing death are arrested and convicted, and those who help these same people to die remain unpunished.

Does all this sound like a dystopian scenario that has nothing to do with Croatia? In July 2012, for the first time in recent Croatian history, something similar occurred, although with a better outcome than in Italy. In the waters south of the island of Mljet, a boat without a driver was sighted, in which 65 Asian-African immigrants were sheltered. Having set sail from Greece, and due to engine failure, the ship had spent two days drifting at sea. The immigrants were originally from Somalia, Egypt, Syria and Afghanistan, and they wanted to be deployed on the Italian coast. Eventually they were brought into the port of Dubrovnik, where they were assisted. What this case shows in not only the quick reaction of the Croatian coast guard, but also the unpreparedness of the Croatian authorities, who have not yet built a reception centre in Dubrovnik and who continually sweep the issue of immigration under the carpet. Croatia is, in fact, the EU country with the longest land border with countries that are not members; somewhat longer than that of Finland/Russia (1.340 km) and Greece/Turkey (1.248 km). Much of this boarder is shared with Bosnia and Herzegovina, Serbia and Montenegro. And instead of Italy, which is quite successful, and even violent, at fighting waves of immigrants, Croatian waters could easily become a new route for immigrants in search of the EU.

What is happening here again reveals the hypocrisy of the

European Union. The first reaction of the Italian government to the revolution in Tunisia in 2011, was to send additional Navy units around Lampedusa in order to prevent a wave of new immigrants. Following the war that broke out in Libya (and initiated by France), the French Prime Minister Francois Fillon announced that France has liberated Benghazi and sent two planes of medical aid. At first glance, this seems like a wonderful gesture of solidarity, but do you know what Fillon's explanation was? That this was one of the measures taken to stop the wave of immigrants that threatens Mediterranean countries. As a result of the conflict in Libya, almost a million people sought refuge in Tunisia, Egypt, Chad and Niger, while the European Union – which is supposedly fighting for 'human rights' in Libya and other African-Arab countries adopted a repressive approach through the agency for border control, *Frontex,* which intercepted migrants and often left them to drown. The war in Libya is supposedly over, but the war against immigrants continues. Since then, an average of 1500 immigrants die every year in the Mediterranean.

Until now, Slovenia was the one who 'regulated' their neighbours (and the whole of the Balkans) at the border to the EU, but now it seems that Croatia will once again become the 'antemurale Europae', reminding us of its role as 'Antemurale Christianitatis', a title that was given to Croatia in 1519 by Pope Leo X, in praise of its struggle against the Turks. Realising that title anew before its entrance to the EU, Croatia has introduced a visa for Turkish citizens, as required by the EU, and causing Turkey to reciprocate in turn, by re-introduced visas for Croatian citizens. However, as in the cases of Romania and Bulgaria, we should know that joining the EU does not necessarily mean entering the 'Schengen' zone. This is best confirmed by none other than Manuel Barroso, when at the end of 2012 he gave an interview to the

Frankfurter Allgemeine Zeitung titled 'We need more Europe'. In addition to the interview there was a small, barely noticeable piece of news: 'Romania is still not included in the Schengen zone.' In short, as the terrified residents of Dugave stated 'the Blacks are coming!' and the residents of the European Union are already fearful, knowing that 'the Croats are coming!' Well, you know that when someone comes directly from Croatia to a European metropolis, s/he just stands out. Dressed in traditional Croatian clothes, and speaking a mostly incomprehensible language, they roam the streets, shouting to each other like they are in the bush ...

SLAVOJ ŽIŽEK

13

SHOPLIFTERS OF THE WORLD UNITE

Repetition, according to Hegel, plays a crucial role in history: when something happens just once, it may be dismissed as an accident, something that might have been avoided if the situation had been handled differently; but when the same event repeats itself, it is a sign that a deeper historical process is unfolding. When Napoleon lost at Leipzig in 1813, it looked like bad luck; when he lost again at Waterloo, it was clear that his time was over. The same holds for the continuing financial crisis. In September 2008, it was presented by some as an anomaly that could be corrected through better regulations etc; now that signs of a repeated financial meltdown are gathering it is clear that we are dealing with a structural phenomenon.

We are told again and again that we are living through a debt crisis, and that we all have to share the burden and tighten our belts. All, that is, except the (very) rich. The idea of taxing them more is taboo: if we did, the argument runs, the rich would have no incentive to invest, fewer jobs would be created and we would all suffer. The only way to save ourselves from hard times is for the poor to get poorer and the rich to get richer. What should the poor do? What *can* they do?

Although the riots in the UK were triggered by the suspicious shooting of Mark Duggan, everyone agrees that they express a deeper unease – but of what kind? As with the car burnings in the Paris banlieues in 2005, the UK rioters had no message to deliver. (There is a clear contrast with the massive student demonstrations in November 2010, which also turned to violence. The students were making clear that they rejected the proposed reforms to higher education.) This is why it is difficult to conceive of the UK rioters in Marxist terms, as an instance of the emergence of the revolutionary subject; they fit much better the Hegelian notion of the 'rabble', those outside organised social space, who can express their discontent only through 'irrational' outbursts of destructive violence – what Hegel called 'abstract negativity'.

There is an old story about a worker suspected of stealing: every evening, as he leaves the factory, the wheelbarrow he pushes in front of him is carefully inspected. The guards find nothing; it is always empty. Finally, the penny drops: what the worker is stealing are the wheelbarrows themselves. The guards were missing the obvious truth, just as the commentators on the riots have done. We are told that the disintegration of the communist regimes in the early 1990s signalled the end of ideology: the time of large-scale ideological projects culminating in totalitarian catastrophe was over; we had entered a new era of rational, pragmatic politics. If the commonplace that we live in a post-ideological era is true in any sense, it can be seen in this recent outburst of violence. This was zero-degree protest, a violent action demanding nothing. In their desperate attempt to find meaning in the riots, the sociologists and editorial-writers obfuscated the enigma the riots presented.

The protesters, though underprivileged and de facto socially excluded, weren't living on the edge of starvation.

People in much worse material straits, let alone conditions of physical and ideological oppression, have been able to organise themselves into political forces with clear agendas. The fact that the rioters have no programme is therefore itself a fact to be interpreted: it tells us a great deal about our ideological-political predicament and about the kind of society we inhabit, a society which celebrates choice but in which the only available alternative to enforced democratic consensus is a blind acting out. Opposition to the system can no longer articulate itself in the form of a realistic alternative, or even as a utopian project, but can only take the shape of a meaningless outburst. What is the point of our celebrated freedom of choice when the only choice is between playing by the rules and (self-)destructive violence?

Alain Badiou has argued that we live in a social space which is increasingly experienced as 'worldless': in such a space, the only form protest can take is meaningless violence. Perhaps this is one of the main dangers of capitalism: although by virtue of being global it encompasses the whole world, it sustains a 'worldless' ideological constellation in which people are deprived of their ways of locating meaning. The fundamental lesson of globalisation is that capitalism can accommodate itself to all civilisations, from Christian to Hindu or Buddhist, from West to East: there is no global 'capitalist worldview', no 'capitalist civilisation' proper. The global dimension of capitalism represents truth without meaning.

The first conclusion to be drawn from the riots, therefore, is that both conservative and liberal reactions to the unrest are inadequate. The conservative reaction was predictable: there is no justification for such vandalism; one should use all necessary means to restore order; to prevent further explosions of this kind we need not more tolerance and social help but more discipline, hard work and a sense of responsibility. What's wrong with this account is not only that it ignores the desperate social situation pushing young people towards violent outbursts but, perhaps more important, that it ignores the way these outbursts echo the hidden premises of conservative ideology itself. When, in the 1990s, the Conservatives launched their 'back to basics' campaign, its obscene complement was revealed by Norman Tebbit: 'Man is not just a social but also a territorial animal; it must be part of our agenda to satisfy those basic instincts of tribalism and territoriality.' This is what 'back to basics' was really about: the unleashing of the barbarian who lurked beneath our apparently civilised, bourgeois society, through the satisfying of the barbarian's 'basic instincts'. In the 1960s, Herbert Marcuse introduced the concept of 'repressive desublimation' to explain the 'sexual revolution': human drives could be desublimated, allowed free rein, and still be subject to capitalist control – viz, the porn industry. On British streets during the unrest, what we saw was not men reduced to 'beasts', but the stripped-down form of the 'beast' produced by capitalist ideology.

Meanwhile leftist liberals, no less predictably, stuck to their mantra about social programmes and integration initiatives, the neglect of which has deprived second and third-generation immigrants of their economic and social prospects: violent outbursts are the only means they have to articulate their dissatisfaction. Instead of indulging ourselves in revenge fantasies, we should make the effort to understand the deeper causes of the outbursts. Can we even imagine what it means to be a young man in a poor, racially mixed area, a priori suspected and harassed by the police, not only unemployed but often unemployable, with no hope of a future? The implication is that the conditions these people find themselves in make it inevitable that they will take to the streets. The problem with this account, though, is that it lists only the objective conditions for the riots. To riot is to make a subjective statement, implicitly to declare how one relates to one's objective conditions.

We live in cynical times, and it's easy to imagine a protester who, caught looting and burning a store and pressed for his reasons, would answer in the language used by social workers and sociologists, citing diminished social mobility, rising insecurity, the disintegration of paternal authority, the lack of maternal love in his early childhood. He knows what he is doing, then, but is doing it nonetheless.

It is meaningless to ponder which of these two reactions, conservative or liberal, is the worse: as Stalin would have put it, they are *both* worse, and that includes the warning given by both sides that the real danger of these outbursts resides in the predictable racist reaction of the 'silent majority'. One of the forms this reaction took was the 'tribal' activity of the local (Turkish, Caribbean, Sikh) communities which quickly organised their own vigilante units to protect their property. Are the shopkeepers a small bourgeoisie defending their property against a genuine, if violent, protest against the system; or are they representatives of the working class, fighting the forces of social disintegration? Here too one should reject the demand to take sides. The truth is that the conflict was between two poles of the underprivileged: those who have succeeded in functioning within the system versus those who are too frustrated to go on trying. The rioters' violence was almost exclusively directed against their own. The cars burned and the shops looted were not in rich neighbourhoods, but in the rioters' own. The conflict is not between different parts of society; it is, at its most radical, the conflict between society and society, between those with everything, and those with nothing, to lose; between those with no stake in their community and those whose stakes are the highest.

Zygmunt Bauman characterised the riots as acts of 'defective and disqualified consumers': more than anything else, they were a manifestation of a consumerist desire violently enacted when unable to realise itself in the 'proper' way – by shopping. As such, they also contain a moment of genuine protest, in the form of an ironic response to consumerist ideology: 'You call on us to consume while simultaneously depriving us of the means to do it properly – so here we are doing it the only way we can!' The riots are a demonstration of the material force of ideology – so much, perhaps, for the 'post-ideological society'. From a revolutionary point of view, the problem with the riots is not the violence as such, but the fact that the violence is not truly self-assertive. It is impotent rage and despair masked as a display of force; it is envy masked as triumphant carnival.

The riots should be situated in relation to another type of violence that the liberal majority today perceives as a threat to our way of life: terrorist attacks and suicide bombings. In both instances, violence and counter-violence are caught up in a vicious circle, each generating the forces it tries to combat. In both cases, we are dealing with blind *passages à l'acte*, in which violence is an implicit admission of impotence. The difference is that, in contrast to the riots in the UK or in Paris, terrorist attacks are carried out in service of the absolute Meaning provided by religion.

But weren't the Arab uprisings a collective act of resistance that avoided the false alternative of self-destructive violence and religious fundamentalism? Unfortunately, the Egyptian summer of 2011 will be remembered as marking the end of revolution, a time when its emancipatory potential was suffocated. Its gravediggers are the army and the Islamists. The contours of the pact between the army (which is Mubarak's army) and the Islamists (who were marginalised in the early months of the upheaval but are now gaining ground) are increasingly clear: the Islamists will tolerate the army's material privileges and in exchange will secure ideological hegemony. The losers will be the pro-Western liberals, too weak – in spite of the CIA funding they are getting – to 'promote democracy', as well as the true agents of the spring events, the emerging secular left that has been trying to set up a network of civil society organisations, from trade unions to feminists. The rapidly worsening economic situation will sooner or later bring the poor, who were largely absent from the spring protests, onto the streets. There is likely to be a new explosion, and the difficult question for Egypt's political subjects is who will succeed in directing the rage of the poor? Who will translate it into a political programme: the new secular left or the Islamists?

The predominant reaction of Western public opinion to the pact between Islamists and the army will no doubt be a triumphant display of cynical wisdom: we will be told that, as the case of (non-Arab) Iran made clear, popular upheavals in Arab countries always end in militant Islamism. Mubarak will appear as having been a much lesser evil – better to stick with the devil you know than to play around with emancipation. Against such cynicism, one should remain unconditionally faithful to the radical-emancipatory core of the Egypt uprising.

But one should also avoid the temptation of the narcissism of the lost cause: it's too easy to admire the sublime beauty of uprisings doomed to fail. Today's left faces the problem of 'determinate negation': what new order should replace the old one after the uprising, when the sublime enthusiasm of the first moment is over? In this context, the manifesto of the

Spanish *indignados*, issued after their demonstrations in May, is revealing. The first thing that meets the eye is the pointedly apolitical tone: 'Some of us consider ourselves progressive, others conservative. Some of us are believers, some not. Some of us have clearly defined ideologies, others are apolitical, but we are all concerned and angry about the political, economic and social outlook that we see around us: corruption among politicians, businessmen, bankers, leaving us helpless, without a voice.' They make their protest on behalf of the 'inalienable truths that we should abide by in our society: the right to housing, employment, culture, health, education, political participation, free personal development and consumer rights for a healthy and happy life.' Rejecting violence, they call for an 'ethical revolution. Instead of placing money above human beings, we shall put it back to our service. We are people, not products. I am not a product of what I buy, why I buy and who I buy from.' Who will be the agents of this revolution? The *indignados* dismiss the entire political class, right and left, as corrupt and controlled by a lust for power, yet the manifesto nevertheless consists of a series of demands addressed at – whom? Not the people themselves: the *indignados* do not (yet) claim that no one else will do it for them, that they themselves have to be the change they want to see. And this is the fatal weakness of recent protests: they express an authentic rage which is not able to transform itself into a positive programme of socio-political change. They express a spirit of revolt without revolution.

The situation in Greece looks more promising, probably owing to the recent tradition of progressive self-organisation (which disappeared in Spain after the fall of the Franco regime). But even in Greece, the protest movement displays the limits of self-organisation: protesters sustain a space of egalitarian freedom with no central authority to regulate it, a public space where all are allotted the same amount of time to speak and so on. When the protesters started to debate what to do next, how to move beyond mere protest, the majority consensus was that what was needed was not a new party or a direct attempt to take state power, but a movement whose aim is to exert pressure on political parties. This is clearly not enough to impose a reorganisation of social life. To do that, one needs a strong body able to reach quick decisions and to implement them with all necessary harshness.

Srećko Horvat

14
DO MARKETS HAVE FEELINGS?

Even in 1936, in his major work *The General Theory of Employment, Interest and Money*, Keynes imagined a fictional newspaper contest in which participants have to choose from a hundred photographs six most beautiful women. The winner is the one whose six pictures come closest to the most popular combination of all participants' choices. 'It is not about how to choose the ones that are, according to the best personal assessment of the competitors really the prettiest, nor those which the average opinion genuinely considers the most beautiful. Rather, we are concerned with third option in which we dedicate our mind to predicting the average competitors expected average of opinion.' The trick, then, is not to choose the women who we think are the most beautiful, but to try to anticipate what others consider beautiful. According to Keynes, it's a similar situation in the stock exchange: the winner is not the one that makes the greatest investment, but the one that understands the psychology of the masses, which is to say the other players. In other words, the price of a stock is not determined by its fundamental value, but rather by the opinion of others as to the value of those shares.

Over the seventy years that have passed since Keynes' thought experiment, capitalism has gone through several stages, while today it is completely dominated by so-called 'Financialisation'. In short, what we have today is an economy that is not based solely on the financial sector, but one where the financial sector is impossible to separate from the language. Swiss economist Christian Marazzi shows that language is now essential for the functioning (and crisis) of today's capitalism, that the so-called 'Financialisation' functions solely through communication, while the Italian philosopher Franco Berardi Bifo coined the term 'semio-capitalism' to indicate the mode of production in which capital accumulation is achieved mainly through the production and accumulation of characters (hence the 'semi-'), which then produce value. Just look at any 'brokerage' film, from the cult of *Wall Street* to the recent *Margin Call*, in order to see that the buying and selling of stocks depends largely on rumours, speculation and reputation, and that without communication there is no accumulation. Take Greece: even though in substantive terms nothing has changed, except that a government came into power (New Democracy) that has accepted international loans, after the 2012 election we could again hear the stories of 'positive responses in the Stock Exchange' as well as 'the most desired outcomes of the market'. Similar things happen after each Euro-Summit. Markets today are becoming like human beings: they have 'expectations', can 'see', and above all 'react' simply on the basis of words.

If the banking scandal of summer 2012 (under the title of *Libor* – London Interbank Offered Rate) taught us anything, it's not that banks ruthlessly rigged interest charges on each other when borrowing money, nor the revelation that banks manipulate business information and credit rating, and that apart from the British bank Barclay's, other banks such as

UBS, Citigroup, Deutsche Bank, HSBC and JP Morgan Chase are very much involved in the story. We already knew that. The real story of *Libor* is nicely summed up by a text which appeared in the *Wall Street Journal*, and whose title says it all: 'Libor and the destruction of trust.' Yes, the markets in addition to all of those previously mentioned characteristics, are also dealing with 'trust'. The main thesis of this article is the need to go back to a 'real' economy. The problem, however, is that there is now no difference between the 'real' and 'fictitious' sectors, with the best proof being precisely *Libor* itself; not only because the markets have now 'lost confidence', but because *Libor* loans determine how banks approve end-users, making this scandal very much to do with 'real life', in that it affects loans for homes and cars. In short, *Libor* is much more important than at first seems, perhaps even more important than Higgs-boson, news of which – accidentally or not – flooded the world's press at the same time.

More than anything else, including Keynes' experiment, an old film in which Peter Sellers played the role of a lifetime can probably best illustrate this current phase of semio-capitalism. In the film *Being There* (Hal Ashby, 1979) Sellers plays a gardener who cannot read or write, who after the death of his employers has to leave his home and enter 'real life'. Out on the street, he is hit by the car of a wealthy woman, and thinking he was a shrewd businessman, she takes him back her home, where she lives with her wealthy, older husband. At dinner, the wealthy lobbyist asks Sellers, 'What are your plans now Mr Gardener?', to which he honestly replies, 'I would like to work in the garden'. Thinking this is a metaphor, the interlocutor concludes, 'Is not a true businessman working with seeds that would be productive.' By chance, Sellers later finds himself in the company of an American president, where once again his story about gardening is perceived as ingenious metaphor for the economy, 'In the garden, growth has its season. First comes spring and summer, but then fall and winter. And then spring and summer again.' That is precisely the point at which we find ourselves today. The current phase of financial capitalism completely abolished the distinction between 'fiction' and 'real' gardening and business, and we pay the price in our very real lives.

And here we can find a valid response in the famous reply by Humpty Dumpty to Alice's question, 'How can you make a word that means so many different things?' to which he replies, 'The question is which is the Lord, and that's all.' If one paraphrases this response, one could say that financial capitalism works by having authority over meaning; whereby through speculation, reputation, and even rumours, value is created. Aren't the recent Greek elections the best evidence that the real question is 'which is the Lord?' After Greece secured a place in the quarter-finals with Germany at the European Football Championship, the popular joke asked whether Angela Merkel told the Greeks how many goals to let through. That many a true word is spoken in jest was confirmed at the Greek elections. Just the weekend before, the *German Financial Times*, setting a new practice in Germany and the international press, published an article in the Greek language, entitled 'Resist the demagogue', and warning Greek voters not to vote for the left-wing party, SYRIZA. With this, Angela Merkel told them not to vote for those who would not fulfil the agreement with Brussels and admitted that the imposed austerity measures in Greece should serve as an example for the whole eurozone. German Finance Minister, Wolfgang Schäuble joined her and advised the Greeks who to vote for. He further added that while he had great sympathy with the sufferings of the common man, he did not see an alternative to 'tightening their belts'. Manuel Barroso, sent out the same message when, as early as May, he resolutely declared that 'austerity measures have no alternative,' while George Osborne warned of 'dire consequences if Greece leaves the eurozone'. The British historian, Niall Ferguson, even went so far to compare the situation in Greece with the Cuban Missile Crisis.

The day after the elections, newspapers triumphantly raved, 'Disaster Avoided', 'Europe is saved', and 'The world is relieved', while not shying away from phrases such as 'positive responses from stock markets around the world' and 'the outcome that the markets most wanted to see'. At the same time, at the G20 meeting in Mexico, the then Italian Prime Minister, Mario Monti, welcomed the victory of New Democracy, adding that 'it allows us to imagine a more optimistic future for Europe and the euro.' Indeed, these headlines and Monti's message clearly show us in whose interests the forming of a pro-European government in Greece really was. Immediately after the election results, the euro rose to the highest level in that month, while growth was also felt in the Asian and American stock exchanges. The battle was not won by Europe or Greece – the battle was won by the markets. As always. But did SYRIZA really lose? Firstly, we should remember that in the 2009 elections, SYRIZA had only 4 percent of the vote, while only a few years later, it won 17 percent, and in the last election it gained 27 percent. Secondly, we should be aware that the New Democracy party won just 3 percent more votes. In this context, is not all the demagogic force of the German and international media, along with the politicians and bankers, also the best proof that – to paraphrase the Communist Manifesto – 'all the European powers already recognised SYRIZA as a force.' In other words, isn't SYRIZA's success or failure the best indicator that the time for austerity measures is ticking away rapidly but not rapidly enough? And is the point of the thesis put forward by Paul Krugman; that it might not be a bad thing that SYRIZA didn't form a government, because if the current austerity policy – according to the American Nobel Prize winner and the theories of other (not just Keynesian) economists – experiences a complete fiasco, the new Greek government will be discredited in the end and it is in some ways better than if the fault lies with the 'radicals'. Yet what is really radical, are the underlying austerity measures that are dragging down Spain and Portugal and Ireland, and that despite their clear failure, are being further implemented and imposed.

In the last interview with Jacques Derrida, given just two months before his death, he nicely summarised today's problem of Europe: 'Europe is under an obligation to take on a new responsibility. I'm not talking about the European Union as it is today, or the one conceived by today's neo-liberal majority, but a Europe that is coming.' Although it did not win, it was SYRIZA that heralded a new direction. And if nothing else, that has shown that even if we don't achieve political change, then at least a discursive change, in order to say, 'No, we will not pay!' Even the director of the European Central Bank, Mario Draghi, now admits that a 'fiscal pact' will not work without a 'development pact', while the director of the IMF, Christine Lagarde, warns that one should choose the right balance between austerity and growth. What the elections in Greece have shown is that austerity measures do not lead to growth, moreover, that 'structural reforms' could endanger the stability of not only the country that is affected by them (remember the picture of the 77-year-old pensioner killed in April 2012 at Syntagma Square in front of parliament), but of the entire eurozone as such (is it not paradoxical that it is precisely because of the austerity measures the EU is losing its geopolitical position, clearly illustrated by the Greek port of Piraeus losing its business to China?).

What the Greek elections showed us, on the one hand, was the end of the neoliberal consensus (because such was SYRIZA's success that it proved the objection to the eagerly implemented austerity measures and advocated the revision of the debt), while on the other hand it proved the rise of fascism, and even its legalisation under parliamentary democracy. A no less important lesson from the Greek elections is that the direct democracy that was practiced in Syntagma and during the 'occupation' in New York City and beyond is no longer sufficient. It is necessary in order to create pressure and for people to confirm the weakness of representative democracy through direct action, but to a priori cancel each parliamentary struggle in this way can also pave the way for the fascists. And here we have a kind of paradox: SYRIZA would not have managed to win so many votes if it were not for direct democracy and the whole movement on the streets and shops of Greek cities these last few years, nor can austerity measures be stopped only with protests. We need both; which takes us right back to Derrida, who – at a time when the phrase almost sounds like a curse or a bad joke – doesn't hesitate to use the words 'We Europeans', without meaning 'the creation of Europe as a military superpower, protecting the market and the other half in balance with other geopolitical blocks, but rather to a Europe that will sow the seeds of a new post-globalisation politics.'

Should that 'Europe that is coming' then be seen as 'the democracy which is to come' ('*la démocratie à venir*')? If there are two types of future, as Derrida believes, '*la future*' – that future that is in some ways predictable and expected, and '*l'avenir*', one that is totally unexpected and therefore the only real future, then Europe should be viewed from two perspectives. One that is predictable – 'present-day Europe' – is the Europe of further austerity measures, the changing of collective agreements, of new privatisation, layoffs, falling purchasing power, the abolition of the welfare state, etc. 'Europe that is still to come' would be, according to Derrida '*la démocratie à venir*', not some future Europe that will one day be 'present', because that Europe cannot exist in the present, but a Europe that is in accordance with the ambiguity of this perceived future (the plain foreseeable future tense and '*l'avenir*' which literally means 'to come'), just like the Messiah who comes both for the first time and is returning. It is the unpredictable future, the only real future, but it is also the idea of Europe, which despite all the neo-liberal distortions still means or can mean something, or as Derrida says in *L'Autre cap. Suivi de La Démocratie ajourné* (1991) *it* is the 'name of Europe' which, despite Eurocentric illusions and pretensions, is still worth fighting for, 'bearing in mind the tradition of the Enlightenment, but also an awareness of guilt and responsibility for the totalitarian, genocidal and colonial crimes of the past.' The future of Europe now lies in a choice between that simple future tense and that '*l'avenir*', the arrival of Europe which, despite the inability of anticipation as the true guarantor of true future, is nevertheless anticipated and expected.

SLAVOJ ŽIŽEK

15

THE COURAGE TO CANCEL
THE DEBT

Maurizio Lazzarato[45] provides a detailed analysis of how, in
today's global capitalism, debt works across a whole range of
social practices and levels (from nation states down to
individuals). The hegemonic neoliberal ideology endeavours
to extend the logic of market competition to all areas of social
life, so that, for example, health and education, or even
political decisions (voting) themselves, are perceived as investments made by the individual in his or her individual capital.
In this way, the worker is no longer conceived merely as labour
power, but as personal capital making good or bad 'investment'
decisions as s/he moves from job to job and increases or
decreases his/her capital value. This reconceptualisation of the
individual as an 'entrepreneur-of-the-self' means a significant
change in the nature of governance: a move away from the
relative passivity and enclosure of disciplinary regimes (the
school, the factory, the prison), as well as from the bio-
political treatment of the population (by the Welfare State).
How can one govern individuals who are conceived as autonomous agents of free market choices, i.e. as 'entrepreneurs-
of-the-self'? Governance is now exercised at the level of the
environment in which people make their apparently

autonomous decisions: risks are outsourced from companies and states to individuals. Through this individualisation of social policy and privatisation of social protection through its alignment with market norms, protection becomes conditional (no longer a right) and is tied to individuals whose behaviours are thus opened up for evaluation. For the majority of people, being an 'entrepreneur-of-the-self' refers to the individual's ability to deal with outsourced risks without having the necessary resources or power to do so adequately:

> contemporary neo-liberal policies produce a human capital or 'entrepreneur-of-the-self' more or less indebted and more or less poor but always precarious. For the majority of the population, becoming an entrepreneur-of-the-self is limited to managing one's employability, one's debts, the drop in one's salary and income and the reduction in social services according to business and competitive norms.[46]

As individuals become poorer through the shrinkage of their salary and the removal of social provision, neo-liberalism offers them compensation through debt and by promotion of shareholding. In this way, wages or deferred salaries (pensions) don't rise, but people have access to consumer credit and are encouraged to provide for retirement through personal share portfolios; people no longer have a right to housing but have access to housing/mortgage credit; people no longer have a right to higher education, but can take out student loans; mutual and collective protection against risks are dismantled, but people are encouraged to take out private insurances. Without replacing all existing social relationships, the creditor-debt nexus thus comes to overlay them: workers become indebted workers (having to pay back their company shareholders for employing them); consumers become indebted consumers; citizens become indebted citizens, having to take responsibility for their share of their country's debt.

Lazzarato relies here on Nietzsche's idea, developed in his *On the Genealogy of Morals*, that what distinguished human societies, as they moved away from their primitive origins, was their capacity to produce a human able to promise to pay others back and to recognise their debt towards the group. This promise grounds a particular type of memory oriented to the future ('I remember I owe you, so I will behave in ways that will allow me to pay you back'), and thus becomes a way of governing future conducts. In more primitive social groups, debts to others were limited and could be discharged, while with the coming of empires and monotheisms, one's social or divine debt become effectively unpayable. Christianity perfected this mechanism: its all-powerful God meant a debt that was infinite; at the same time, one's guilt for non-payment was internalised. The only way one could possibly repay in any way was through obedience: to the will of God, to the church. Debt, with its grip on past and future behaviours and with its moral reach was a formidable governmental tool – all that remained was for it to be secularised.

This constellation gives rise to a specific type of subjectivity characterised by moralisation and specific temporalisation. The indebted subject practices two kinds of work: salaried labour as well as the work upon the self that is needed to produce a subject who is able to promise, to repay debts, and who is ready to assume guilt for being an indebted subject. A particular set of temporalities are associated with indebtedness: to be able to repay (to remember one's promise), one has to make one's behaviour predictable, regular and calculating. This not only militates against any future revolt with its inevitable disruption of the capacity to repay – it also implies an erasure of the memory of past rebellions and collective resistances with their lot of disrupted time and unpredictable behaviours. This indebted subject is constantly opened up to the evaluating inspection of others: individualised appraisals and targets at work, credit ratings, individual interviews for those in receipt of benefits or public credits. The subject is thus compelled not only to show that he or she will be able to repay debt (and to repay society through the right behaviours), he or she also has to show the right attitudes and assume individual guilt for any failings. This is where the asymmetry between creditor and debtor becomes palpable: the indebted 'entrepreneur-of-the-self' is more active than the subject of the previous more disciplinary modes of governance; however, deprived as s/he is of the ability to govern his or her time, or to evaluate his or her own behaviours, his or her capacity of autonomous action is strictly curtailed.

In case it might seem that debt is simply a governmental tool suited to modulating the behaviour of individuals, it should be noted that similar techniques can apply to the governance of institutions and countries. Anyone following the unfolding, slow motion car crash that is the current crisis could not but be aware of how countries and institutions are under constant evaluation (by credit rating agencies for example), have to accept moral fault for their previous errors and self-indulgence and have to commit to future good behaviour that will ensure that, no matter what cuts have to be made in the body of their social provision, or their workers' rights, they will be able to repay the lending agent's pound of flesh.[47]

The ultimate triumph of capitalism thus occurs when each worker becomes its own capitalist, the 'entrepreneur-of-the-self' who decides how much to invest in his/her own future (education, health, etc.), paying for these investments by getting indebted. The rights (to education, healthcare, housing, etc.) thus become free decisions to invest which are formally at the same level as the banker's or capitalist's decision to invest in this or that company, so that, at this formal level, everyone is a capitalist getting indebted in order to invest. We are here a step further from the formal equality between the capitalist and the worker in the eyes of the law – now they are both capitalist investors; however, the same difference in the 'physiognomy of our dramatis personae' which, according to Marx, appears after the exchange between labour and capital is concluded, re-appears here between the capitalist investor proper and the worker who is compelled to act as the 'entrepreneur-of-the-self': 'The one smirks self-importantly and is intent on business; the other is timid and holds back, like someone who has brought his own hide to market and has nothing else to expect but — a tanning.'[48] And he is right to remain timid – the freedom of choice imposed on him is a false one, it is the very form of his servitude.

How does today's rise of the indebted man, specific to conditions of global capitalism, relate to the relationship of debtor/creditor as a universal anthropological constant articulated by Nietzsche? It is the paradox of direct realisation which turns into its opposite. Today's global capitalism brings the relationship of debtor/creditor to its extreme and simultaneously undermines it: debt becomes an openly ridiculous excess. We thus enter the domain of obscenity: when a credit is accorded, the debtor is not even expected to return it – debt is directly treated as a means of control and domination. Recall the ongoing EU pressure on Greece to implement austerity measures – this pressure fits perfectly what psychoanalysis calls superego. Superego is not an ethical agency proper, but a sadistic agent which bombards the subject with impossible demands, obscenely enjoying the subject's failure to comply with them; the paradox of the superego is that, as Freud saw it clearly, the more we obey its demands, the more we feel guilty. Imagine a vicious teacher who gives his pupils impossible tasks, and then sadistically jeers when he sees their anxiety and panic. This is what is so terribly wrong with the EU demands/commands: they don't even give Greece a chance, the Greek failure is part of the game. The goal of politico-economic analysis is here to deploy strategies of how to step out of this infernal circle of debt and guilt.

A similar paradox was operative from the very beginning, of course, since a promise/obligation which cannot ever be fully met is at the very base of the banking system. When one puts money into a bank, the bank obliges itself to return the money at any point – but we all know that, while the bank can do this to some of the people who deposited money into it, it by definition cannot do it to all of them. However, this paradox which originally held for the relationship between individuals who deposit money and their bank now also holds for the relationship between the bank and (legal or physical) persons who borrowed money from the bank. What this implies is that the true aim of lending money to the debtor is not to get the debt reimbursed with a profit, but the indefinite continuation of the debt which keeps the debtor in permanent dependency and subordination. A decade or so ago, Argentina decided to repay its debt to the IMF ahead of time (with financial help from Venezuela), and the reaction of the IMF was surprising – instead of being glad that it got its money back, the IMF (or, rather, its top representatives) expressed their worry that Argentina will use this new freedom and financial independence from international financial institutions to abandon tight financial politics and engage in careless spending. This uneasiness made palpable the true stakes of the debtor/creditor relationship: debt is an instrument to control and regulate the debtor, and, as such, it strives for its own expanded reproduction.

Another surprise here is that theology and poetry knew this long ago – yet another confirmation of Berardi's topic 'poetry and finance.' Let us jump back to early modernity – why was the story of Orpheus THE opera topic in the first century of its history, when there were almost one hundred recorded versions of it? The figure of Orpheus asking Gods to bring him back his Euridice stands for an intersubjecive constellation which provides as it were the elementary matrix of the opera, more precisely, of the operatic aria: the relationship of the subject (in both senses of the term: auto- nomous agent as well as the subject of legal power) to his Master (Divinity, King, or the Lady of courtly love) is revealed through the hero's song (the counterpoint to the collectivity embodied in the chorus), which is basically a supplication addressed to the Master, a call to him to show mercy, to make an exception, or otherwise forgive the hero his trespass. The first, rudimentary, form of subjectivity is this voice of the subject beseeching the Master to suspend, for a brief moment, his own Law. A dramatic tension in subjectivity arises from the ambiguity between power and impotence that pertains to the gesture of grace by means of which the Master answers the subject's entreaty. As to the official ideology, grace expresses the Master's supreme power, the power to rise above one's own law: only a really powerful Master can afford to distribute mercy. What we have here is a kind of symbolic exchange between the human subject and his divine Master: when the subject, the human mortal, by way of his offer of self-sacrifice, surmounts his finitude and attains the divine heights, the Master responds with the sublime gesture of

Grace, the ultimate proof of HIS humanity. Yet this act of grace is at the same time branded by the irreducible mark of a forced empty gesture: the Master ultimately makes a virtue out of necessity, in that he promotes as a free act what he is in any case compelled to do – if he refuses clemency, he takes the risk that the subject's respectful entreaty will turn into open rebellion.

In Gluck's Orpheus from the late 18th century, the denouement is different: after looking back and thus losing Euridice, Orpheus sings his famous aria 'Che faro senza Euridice,' announcing his intention to kill himself. At this precise point of total self-abandonment, Love intervenes and gives him back his Euridice. This specific form of subjectivisation – the intervention of Grace not as a simple answer to the subject's entreaty, but as an answer which occurs in the very moment when the subject decides to put his life at stake, to risk everything – is the twist added by Gluck. What is crucial here is the link between the assertion of subjective autonomy and the 'answer of the Real,' the mercy shown by the big Other: far from being opposed, they rely on each other, i.e. the modern subject can assert its radical autonomy only insofar as it can count on the support of the 'big Other,' only insofar as his autonomy is sustained by the social substance. No wonder this gesture of 'autonomy and mercy,'[49] of mercy intervening at the very point of the subject's assertion of full autonomy, is discernible throughout the history of the opera, from Mozart to Wagner: in Idomeneo and Seraglio, the Other (Neptun, Basha Selim) displays mercy at the very moment when the hero is ready to sacrifice his/her life, and the same happens even twice in The Magic Flute (the magic intervention of the Other prevents both Pamina's and Papageno's suicide); in Fidelio, the trumpet announces the Minister's arrival at the very point when Leonora puts her life at stake to save Florestan; up to Wagner's Parsifal in which Parsifal himself intervenes and redeems Amfortas precisely when Amfortas asks to be stabbed to death by his knights. Of special interest is here Mozart's late opera Clemenza di Tito in which we witness a sublime/ridiculous explosion of mercies – just before the final pardon, Tito himself exasperates at the proliferation of treasons which oblige him to proliferate acts of clemency:

> The very moment that I absolve one criminal, I discover another ... I believe the stars conspire to oblige me, in spite of myself, to become cruel. No: they shall not have this satisfaction. My virtue has already pledged itself to continue the contest. Let us see, which is more constant, the treachery of others or my mercy ... Let it be known to Rome that I am the same and that I know all, absolve everyone, and forget everything.

One can almost hear Tito complaining like Rossini's Figaro: 'Uno per volta, per carita!' – 'Please, not so fast, one after the other, in the line for mercy!' Living up to his task, Tito forgets everyone, but those whom he pardons are condemned to remember it forever:

> SEXTUS: It is true, you pardon me, Emperor; but my heart will not absolve me; it will lament the error until it no longer has memory.
> TITUS: The true repentance of which you are capable, is worth more than constant fidelity.

This couplet from the finale blurts out the obscene secret of Clemenza: the pardon does not really abolish the debt, it rather makes it infinite – we are forever indebted to the person who pardoned us. No wonder Tito prefers repentance to fidelity: in fidelity to the Master, I follow him out of respect, while in repentance, what attached me to the Master is the infinite indelible guilt. In this, Tito is a thoroughly Christian master. One usually opposes the Jewish rigorous Justice and the Christian Mercy, the inexplicable gesture of undeserved pardon: we, humans, were born in sin, we cannot ever repay our debts and redeem ourselves through our own acts – our only salvation lies in God's Mercy, in His supreme sacrifice. In this very gesture of breaking the chain of Justice through the inexplicable act of Mercy, of paying our debts, Christianity imposes on us an even stronger debt: we are forever indebted to Christ, we cannot ever repay him for what he did for us. The Freudian name for such an excessive pressure which we cannot ever remunerate is, of course, superego. (One should not forget that the notion of Mercy is strictly correlative to that of Sovereignty: only the bearer of sovereign power can dispense mercy.)[50]

Accordingly, it is Judaism which is conceived as the religion of the superego (of man's subordination to the jealous, mighty and severe God), in contrast to the Christian God of Mercy and Love. However, it is precisely through not demanding from us the price for our sins, through paying this price for us Himself, that the Christian God of Mercy establishes itself as the supreme superego agency: 'I paid the highest price for your sins, and you are thus indebted to me forever ...' The contours of this God as the superego agency, whose very Mercy generates the indelible guilt of believers, are discernible up to Stalin. One should never forget that, as the (now available) minutes of the meetings of the Politburo and Central Committee from the 1930s demonstrate, Stalin's direct interventions were as a rule those of displaying mercy. When younger CC members, eager to prove their revolutionary fervour, demanded instant death penalty for Bukharin, Stalin always intervened and said 'Patience! His guilt is not yet proven!' or something similar. Of course this was a hypocritical attitude – Stalin was well aware that he himself generated the destructive fervour, that the younger members were eager to please him – but, nonetheless, the appearance of mercy is necessary here.

And the same holds for today's capitalism. Referring to George Bataille's notion of the 'general economy' of sovereign expenditure, which he opposes to the 'restrained economy' of capitalism's endless profiteering, Peter Sloterdijk provides (in Zorn und Zeit) the outlines of capitalism's split from itself, its immanent self-overcoming: capitalism culminates when it 'creates out of itself its own most radical – and the only fruitful – opposite, totally different from what the classic Left, caught in its miserabilism, was able to dream about.'[51] His positive mention of Andrew Carnegie shows the way: the sovereign self-negating gesture of the endless accumulation of wealth is to spend this wealth for things beyond price, and outside market circulation: public good, arts and sciences, health, etc. This concluding 'sovereign' gesture enables the capitalist to break out of the vicious cycle of endless expanded reproduction, of gaining money in order to earn more money. When he donates his accumulated wealth to public good, the capitalist self-negates himself as the mere personification of capital and its reproductive circulation: his life acquires meaning. It is no longer just expanded reproduction as self-goal. Furthermore, the capitalist thus accomplishes the shift from Eros to Thymos, from the perverted 'erotic' logic of accumulation to public recognition and reputation. What this amounts to is nothing less than elevating figures like George Soros or Bill Gates to personifications of the inherent self-negation of the capitalist process itself: their work of charity, their immense donations to public welfare, is not just a personal idiosyncrasy, whether sincere or hypocritical, it is the logical concluding point of capitalist circulation, necessary from the strictly economic standpoint, since it allows the capitalist system to postpone its crisis. It re-establishes balance – a kind of redistribution of wealth to the truly needy – without falling into a fateful trap: the destructive logic of resentment and enforced statist redistribution of wealth which can only end in generalised misery. (It also avoids, one might add, the other mode of re-establishing a kind of balance and asserting Thymos through sovereign expenditure, namely wars.)

How, then, does Tito fit into the series of Mozart's operas? The entire canon of Mozart's great operas can be read as the deployment of the motif of pardon, of dispensing mercy, in all its variations: the higher power intervenes with mercy in Idomeneo and Seraglio; in Le nozze di Figaro, the subjects themselves pardon the Count who refuses mercy; etc. In order to grasp properly the place of Clemenza in this series, one should read it together with Zauberflote, as its mocking shadowy double: if Zauberflote is mercy at its most sublime, Clemenza turns this sublimity into a ridiculous excess. The ridiculous proliferation of mercy in Clemenza means that power no longer functions in a normal way, so that it has to be sustained by mercy all the time: if Master has to show mercy, it means that the law failed, that the legal state machinery is not able to run on its own and needs an incessant intervention from the outside. [52]

SREĆKO HORVAT

16

THE EASIEST WAY TO THE GULAG IS TO JOKE ABOUT THE GULAG

'The question is,' said Alice, 'whether you can make words mean so many different things.'

'The question is,' said Humpty Dumpty, 'which is to be master – that is all.'

Lewis Carroll, *Through the Looking-Glass*

According to the Russian historian Roy Medvedev, around 200,000 people in the USSR were sent to a Gulag for telling a joke. When a system is threatened by jokes and jokes are taken too seriously, it is no sign of strength, but exactly the opposite: a clear indication of its weakness. Even if you have the power to send people to a Gulag.

Following the visit of SYRIZA leader Alexis Tsipras to the Zagreb Subversive Festival in May 2013, only two months prior to the accession of Croatia to the European Union, it seems that jokes are to be taken more seriously now than ever. First, the Greek media reported that Hollywood director Oliver Stone openly supported him, saying without hesitation that he hoped Tsipras would become the next Greek prime minister because he represents 'hope for Greece, and he could bring a big change not only for Greece and Europe, but perhaps for the world'. Then, during the same conversation on Greek National Television, Slavoj Žižek added that he also believes in Tsipras, but 'as a Platonist', because 'if philosophers are not kings, then at least you have to control kings', and concluded that he supports him, 'but under the condition I will be his secret advisor'.

This was, of course, a joke. But it was another of his jokes that provoked a harsh reaction from the Greek establishment. During a public debate with Tsipras in Zagreb, 'the most dangerous philosopher in the West', said that in his 'vision of democratic future all the people who do not support SYRIZA would get a one way, first-class ticket to the Gulag'. The Greek media immediately drummed up a furore, prompting Greek prime minister, Antonis Samaras, to describe Žižek's comment as 'horrible and disgusting', bearing in mind that thousands of Greeks were killed in Gulags. And Tsipras was accused of laughing at the joke.

But what exactly did Žižek say in Zagreb? To avoid any new misunderstandings, it is worth quoting the whole passage: 'The fight that SYRIZA is fighting is the fight for the very soul of Europe. And I am here without any shame eurocentrist. OK, it's nice for politically correct reasons to blame Europe for everything – imperialism, colonialism, slavery – but my God, Europe did give, and let's be proud of that, something wonderful to humanity: the idea of radical egalitarianism, of radical democracy, feminism, etc. This is at the core of European identity, and that is at stake today. So as Alexis said – who is the danger? – today's defenders of Europe, Brussels' technocrats or anti-immigrant nationalists, they are the threat to what is worth fighting for in European legacy. SYRIZA is not a Greek phenomenon; SYRIZA is something that is one of the few signs of hope for the whole of Europe ... And the test for the people, when you ask them what they think about Europe is to simply ask them what they think about SYRIZA. If they don't support SYRIZA, then in my vision of democratic future all these people will get a first-class one-way ticket to the Gulag.'[53]

This is a classic Žižek joke and those who follow him have long been accustomed to his sense of humour. However, Tsipras' opponents managed – in the best Stalinist manner – to take the joke out of context and convince those who didn't follow the Zagreb debate that 'Žižek recommends the Gulag for all opponents of SYRIZA.'[54] Yet, the truth is quite opposite.

The same day when Samaras and his 'Truth Team' manu-factured the scandal,[55] the extreme right-wing party, Golden Dawn, which has 18 members in parliament, threatened to organise a march of 100,000 Greeks to prevent the con-struction of a mosque in Athens. Although about 500,000 Muslims reside in Greece, no Greek government has ever really tried to improve the position of the Muslim community in Greek society, and Samaras' government has so far pursued the same path. Nothing was done even when, to prevent the construction of the first mosque in Athens, Golden Dawn sent a letter to the Muslim Association of Greece with the following text: 'Muslim murderers, if you don't close your brothels in Greece by 30 June, we will send you to hell. Those who do not comply with the ultimatum, will be slaughtered like chickens on the road.'[56]

Only a day later, on 21 May 2013, Golden Dawn MP, spokes-person and 'pop star', Elias Kasidiaris, was invited to a radio show together with Adonis Gorgiadis, a New Democracy MP. Gorgiadis defended the use of controversial detention centres for immigrants, claiming that these centres respected the detainees' human rights, and he also accused Golden Dawn of lying when they claim that the illegal migration 'problem' can easily be solved. Kasidiaris answered that these detention centres are in fact too good for immigrants, as they receive food and operate air conditioning; he further declared that were Golden Dawn in government, illegal immigrants would be sent to the Aegean islands which were used as offshore prisons for political prisoners throughout the twentieth century. So much for the Gulag and Samaras accusing Tsipras of laughing at Žižek's joke.

On the one hand, we have Žižek's quip about the 'Gulag', on the other, we have not only harmful words, but concrete action, including physical violence against immigrants and Muslims. And yet, it is the former that creates controversy and feigned outrage, while the latter is quietly accepted and progressively adopted as part of the mainstream political discourse. And isn't a similar trend observable in the whole of Europe? On the one side, it is always SYRIZA that is described as a threat to Europe, becoming the bogeyman we saw in 2012, when right before the Greek elections the German *Financial Times* published an article in Greek to convince voters not to vote for Tsipras. On the other, it is precisely the direction taken by the European Union – unstoppable new austerity measures and privatisations – which is the real cause of increasing unemployment and rising discontents that can easily be mobilised and channelled through new nationalist or openly fascist movements.

In this sense, Golden Dawn is actually the long arm and extension of the system, as Tsipras insisted in Zagreb. During public appearances, Golden Dawn and the like loudly express that which is repressed in the European Union's vocabulary, these new extreme movements create a political climate where, for example, the exceptionally tough anti-immigration legislation of the EU begins to look 'moderate' in comparison. As a consequence, this shifting context enables extreme movements to radicalise further. For example, the electoral slogans used by Hans-Christian Strache in the 2010 Vienna elections *Zu viel Fremdes tut niemanden gut* ('Too much foreign does no one any good') or *Mehr Mut für unser Wiener Blut* ('More strength for our Viennese blood') – are in perfect harmony with the mechanisms that the company Frontex is using to stop the wave of migrants to Europe. The same goes for Golden Dawn's attempt to stop the construction of a mosque in Athens: it is not an exception but rather the confirmation of a general trend across Europe, from the UK and France, to Switzerland, where the construction of minarets was banned in a 2009 referendum.

It is in this sense that Tsipras' Zagreb declaration that, 'the danger for Europe is not SYRIZA, but Angela Merkel' has to be understood. The next day of course, once again drawing on the Hegelian 'bad infinity' of a media manufacturing consent, a Croatian newspaper published a headline announcing: 'Merkel is a danger for Europe, says radical Tsipras'. Because, of course, the idea that the German Chancellor is a danger can only be voiced by such a 'radical', while those whose policies are producing an irresistible rightwards turn in Europe are not described as such.

But the problem is not so much Merkel herself as an old tactic that the Nazis themselves called *Gleichschaltung* ('equalisation'), a term that denotes the process through which the regime forcibly 'equated' various elements of society. Following this logic, all elements which don't fit into the prevailing paradigm – be it left or right – are 'gleich', the same – and undesirable. This is why, in 2012 alone, the leader of SYRIZA was described as a 'naive radical,' a 'dangerous liar', a 'populist demagogue' and 'the most dangerous man in Europe'. The German weekly *Der Spiegel* went so far as to include him in a list of the 'ten most dangerous politicians in Europe'. Here, the *Gleichschaltung* consisted of putting

Tsipras alongside French *Front National*'s Marine Le Pen, leading Finnish nationalist Timo Soini, notorious Austrian extremist Hans-Christian Strache and Dutch right-wing populist, Geert Wilders.

So what we have here is actually one of the best jokes to emerge from the USSR, in which all the potential of *Gleichschaltung* is revealed. Three new arrivals in the Gulag camp start talking about the reasons why they are there. 'I kept showing up for my job five minutes late. They accused me of sabotage', says the first. 'Understandable, but I used to come to work five minutes early. And they accused me of spying', says the second. Both then look at the third prisoner, with an air of eager expectation, knowing that there will be a punch line. 'Ha! I always got to work exactly on time. And they suspected that I owned a Western clock'.

A variation of the joke describes the destiny of three prisoners in a cell in the KGB Headquarters at Dzerzhinsky Square. The first asks the second why he has been imprisoned, and he says, 'Because I criticised Karl Radek'. The first man responds, 'But I am here because I spoke out in favour of Radek!' They turn to the third man who has been sitting quietly at the back, and ask him why he is in jail, too. He responds, 'I'm Karl Radek'.

Doesn't the official reaction of the current Greek government follow remarkably similar lines? Following Žižek's joke, we can easily imagine the following situation. Three prisoners in the Gulag start talking about how they ended up there. The first says, 'I'm here because I fought against immigrants.' Another, 'I'm here because I fought against Samaras'. And finally the third: 'I'm here because I fought against extreme nationalists and Angela Merkel, and they accused of being against the European Union.' The third is, of course, Alexis Tsipras.

The European Union has not yet fallen so far as to develop

a sophisticated legislative system for a structural *Gleich-schaltung*, but the reaction of the EU-approved Samaras Government's 'Truth Team' is a symptom of what is wrong with Europe. The paradox is that those who proclaim themselves to be the 'Truth Team' and fight against politically incorrect jokes (e.g. the Gulag) that recreate the atmosphere described by Medvedev as a situation in which jokes are treated as a threat, while the real threat – the current policies of the Troika and Golden Dawn – is treated as a joke. The paradox is also obvious when it comes to EU policies, which are the real reason behind increasing radicalism all around Europe. To put Tsipras arm in arm with Le Pen or Wilders like *Der Spiegel* has done is not only political falsification, but a cynical way to defend a risky political game that is now becoming the real danger for Europe. In other words: it is not Tsipras who is dangerous, it is *austerity Europe*.

Here is an example from the newest member state of the EU. Only a few days after Margaret Thatcher died, a leading Croatian newspaper published an article echoing the famous Heideggerian motto *Nur noch ein Gott kann uns retten* ('Only a God Can Save Us'). The obituary was written by a former minister of finance during Tuđman's government and the 'Transition-period', who is infamous for declaring that 'privatisation is a very difficult operation, and your suit cannot stay clean. You will come out of it with some stains. But somebody had to do it'. The title of his panegyric was: 'Only a Margaret Thatcher can save Croatia'.[57] We don't need WikiLeaks or historical books to show how Croatia (and other ex-Yugoslavian states) adopted neoliberal reforms. It is sufficient to listen to the protagonists themselves.

So, the economist recalls his first meeting with Margaret Thatcher during her visit to Croatia in September 1998. That was the year when she received the highest state award from president Tuđman, and the economist confessed to her that some of the people in Croatia mock him for being a 'follower of Thatcherism'. 'Beautiful', she said, 'obviously you are doing the right things. Don't give up!' And what are the right things for today's Croatia? According to the economist: 'fiscal consolidation, privatisation of large state-owned enterprises, deregulation, the closure of chronic losers, reforms of the health care system and pensions system, finding the right measures in social tripartism, etc.' And this is not all: 'Our luck is that 'She' did all this and received numerous awards during her life, from her political rivals to the young people who owe their jobs today largely to her once unpopular reforms'. He, of course, forgot to mention that Croatia comes third in Europe when it comes to youth unemployment (around 51.6%), just behind Greece (59.1%) and Spain (55.9%).[58]

As we know, in the interview published in *Der Spiegel* in May, 1976 (but written in 1966) Heidegger was asked 'can the individual man in any way still influence this web of fateful circumstance?', and his answer was the following: 'If I may answer briefly, and perhaps clumsily, but after long reflection: philosophy will be unable to effect any immediate change in the current state of the world. This is true not only of philosophy but of all purely human reflection and endeavour. Only a god can save us. The only possibility available to us is that by thinking and poetising we prepare a readiness for the appearance of a god, or for the absence of a god in (our) decline insofar as in view of the absent god we are in a state of decline.'[59] To do something which might appear as blasphemy for serious Heideggerians, couldn't we read Heidegger *avec* the Croatian economist and imagine the following conclusion: 'If I may answer briefly, and perhaps clumsily, but after long reflection: SYRIZA will be unable to effect any immediate change in the current state of the world. This is true not only of SYRIZA but of all purely human reflection and endeavour. Only Margaret Thatcher can save us. The only possibility available to us is that by thinking and poetising we prepare a readiness for the appearance of a new Margaret Thatcher, or for the absence of Thatcher in (our) decline, insofar as in view of the absent Thatcher we are in a state of decline.' Isn't this the message the Troika constantly repeats? At least, the good news for Croatia is that the newest member state fits perfectly into the EU as it already follows its current political and economic dogmas.

The two events – Margaret Thatcher's death and Alexis Tsipras' visit to Croatia – have shown the extent of ideological hegemony in Europe. While it is clear that Thatcher's legacy in no way proves that she was right and Tsipras should not be dismissed as a 'dangerous extremist', the dominance of the perfectly opposite readings show how far we are from a real understanding of what plagues Europe today. And maybe this is something to be added to the recent debate sparked by Etienne Balibar's article on a new Europe.[60] The old Humpty Dumpty lesson is more relevant than ever: 'The question is which is to be master – that's all'. Or, in other words, for a new Europe to emerge, it is not only sufficient to wait for a solution from the 'bottom up', as Balibar stated, what is needed is a clear and strong position – what is needed is a new hegemony.

Balibar dismissed the chance that a European *New Deal* will come from Ms Merkel, while still being convinced that it will come from Germany. But when one thinks about where the battle for hegemony is being fought today – against modern Gulags and extremist tendencies – it becomes obvious the solution will – and must – come from the European South.

Why? Because the laboratory rabbits – like Greece – from the European South are not only getting accustomed to being the victims of 'shock doctrine' experiments, but are also willing to experiment themselves. And to reply to one of the replies to Etienne Balibar – namely that of Sandro Mezzadra – who is claiming that we need a *founding campaign*, 'capable of transforming existing forces and institutions, creating new ones, channelling social struggles and indignation towards this purpose of building another Europe' – one capable of producing new political languages and cultural imaginaries'[61] – to him and others I say we already have just such a *founding campaign*, and it is something whose name is missing from the whole current debate about re-building Europe. It is called SYRIZA. Of, course, we have to see what will happen with them if they really come to power, but what SYRIZA succeeded to change in a really short time is the discourse – which is already a change in the balance of power.

Slavoj Žižek

17

WE NEED A MARGARET
THATCHER OF THE LEFT

In the last pages of his monumental *Second World War*, Winston Churchill ponders on the enigma of a military decision: after the specialists (economic and military analysts, psychologists, meteorologists) propose their analysis, somebody must assume the simple and for that very reason most difficult act of transposing this complex multitude into a simple 'Yes' or 'No'. We shall attack, we continue to wait ... This gesture, which can never be fully grounded in reasons, is that of a Master. It is for the experts to present the situation in its complexity, and it is for the Master to simplify it into a point of decision.

The Master is needed especially in situations of deep crisis. The function of a Master is to enact an authentic division – a division between those who want to drag on within the old parameters and those who are aware of the necessary change. Such a division, not the opportunistic compromises, is the only path to true unity. Let us take an example which surely is not problematic: France in 1940. Even Jacques Duclos, the second man of the French Communist Party, admitted in a private conversation that if, at that point in time, free elections were to be held in France, Marshal Petain would have won with 90 per cent of the vote. When de Gaulle, in his historic act, refused to acknowledge the capitulation to Germans and continued to resist, he claimed that it was only he, not the Vichy regime, who speaks on behalf of the true France (on behalf of true France as such, not only on behalf of the 'majority of the French'!). What he was saying was deeply true even if it was 'democratically' not only without legitimacy, but clearly opposed to the opinion of the majority of the French people.

Margaret Thatcher, the lady who was not for turning, was such a Master, sticking to her decision which was at first perceived as crazy, gradually elevating her singular madness into an accepted norm. When Thatcher was asked about her greatest achievement, she promptly answered: 'New Labour.' And she was right: her triumph was that even her political enemies adopted her basic economic policies – the true triumph is not the victory over the enemy, it occurs when the enemy itself starts to use your language, so that your ideas form the foundation of the entire field.

So what remains of Thatcher's legacy today? Neoliberal hegemony is clearly falling apart. Thatcher was perhaps the only true Thatcherite – she clearly believed in her ideas. Today's neoliberalism, on the contrary, 'only imagines that it believes in itself and demands that the world should imagine the same thing' (to quote Marx). In short, today, cynicism is openly on display. Recall the cruel joke from Lubitsch's To Be Or Not to Be: when asked about the German concentration camps in the occupied Poland, the responsible Nazi officer 'concentration camp Earnhardt' snaps back: 'We do the concentrating, and the Poles do the camping.'

Does the same not hold for the Enron bankruptcy in January 2002 (as well as on all financial meltdowns that followed), which can be interpreted as a kind of ironic commentary on the notion of a risk society? Thousands of employees who lost their jobs and savings were certainly exposed to a risk, but without any true choice – the risk appeared to them as a blind fate. Those, on the contrary, who effectively did have an insight into the risks as well as a possibility to intervene into the situation (the top managers), minimised their risks by cashing in their stocks and options before the bankruptcy – so it is true that we live in a society of risky choices, but some (the Wall Street managers) do the choosing, while others (the common people paying mortgages) do the risking.

One of the weird consequences of the financial meltdown and the measures taken to counteract it (enormous sums of money to help banks) was the revival in the work of Ayn Rand, the closest one can come to the ideologist of the 'greed is good' radical capitalism – the sales of her magnum opus Atlas Shrugged exploded again. According to some reports, there are already signs that the scenario described in Atlas Shrugged – the creative capitalists themselves going on strike – is enacted. John Campbell, a Republican congressman, said: 'The achievers are going on strike. I'm seeing, at a small level, a kind of protest from the people who create jobs ... who are pulling back from their ambitions because they see how they'll be punished for them.' The absurdity of this reaction is that it totally misreads the situation: most of the gigantic sums of bail-out money is going precisely to the Randian deregulated 'titans' who failed in their 'creative' schemes and thereby brought about the meltdown. It is not the great creative geniuses who are now helping lazy ordinary people, it is the ordinary taxpayers who are helping the failed 'creative geniuses.'

The other aspect of Thatcher's legacy targeted by her leftist critics was her 'authoritarian' form of leadership, her lack of the sense for democratic coordination. Here, however, things are more complex than it may appear. The ongoing popular protests around Europe converge in a series of demands which, in their very spontaneity and obviousness, form a kind of 'epistemological obstacle' to the proper confrontation with the ongoing crisis of our political system. These effectively read as a popularised version of Deleuzian politics: people know what they want, they are able to discover and formulate this, but only through their own continuous engagement and activity. So we need active participatory democracy, not just representative democracy with its electoral ritual which every four years interrupts the voters' passivity; we need the self-organisation of the multitude, not a centralised Leninist Party with the Leader, et cetera.

It is this myth of non-representative direct self-organisation which is the last trap, the deepest illusion that should fall, that is most difficult to renounce. Yes, there are in every revolutionary process ecstatic moments of group solidarity when thousands, hundreds of thousands, together occupy a public place, like on Tahrir Square two years ago. Yes, there are moments of intense collective participation where local communities debate and decide, when people live in a kind of permanent emergency state, taking things into their own hands, with no Leader guiding them. But such states don't last, and 'tiredness' is here not a simple psychological fact, it is a category of social ontology.

The large majority – me included – wants to be passive and rely on an efficient state apparatus to guarantee the smooth running of the entire social edifice, so that we can pursue our work in peace. Walter Lippmann wrote in his Public Opinion (1922) that the herd of citizens must be governed by 'a specialised class whose interests reach beyond the locality' – this elite class is to act as a machinery of knowledge that circumvents the primary defect of democracy, the impossible ideal of the 'Omni-competent citizen'. This is how our democracies function – with our consent: there is no mystery in what Lippmann was saying, it is an obvious fact; the mystery is that, knowing it, we play the game. We act as if we are free and freely deciding, silently not only accepting but even demanding that an invisible injunction (inscribed into the very form of our free speech) tells us what to do and think. 'People know what they want' – no, they don't, and they don't want to know it. They need a good elite, which is why a proper politician does not only advocate people's interests; it is through him that they discover what they 'really want.'

As to the molecular self-organising multitude against the hierarchic order sustained by the reference to a charismatic leader, note the irony of the fact that Venezuela, a country praised by many for its attempts to develop modes of direct democracy (local councils, cooperatives, workers running factories), is also a country whose president was Hugo Chavez, a strong charismatic leader if there ever was one. It is as if the Freudian rule of transference is at work here: in order for the individuals to 'reach beyond themselves,' to break out of the passivity of representative politics and engage themselves as direct political agents, the reference to a leader is necessary, a leader who allows them to pull themselves out of the swamp like baron Munchhausen, a leader who is 'supposed to know' what they want. It is in this sense that Alain Badiou recently pointed out how horizontal networking undermines the classic Master, but it simultaneously breeds new forms of domination which are much stronger than the classic Master. Badiou's thesis is that a subject needs a Master to elevate itself above the 'human animal' and to practice fidelity to a Truth-Event:

The Master is the one who helps the individual to become subject. That is to say, if one admits that the subject emerges

163

in the tension between the individual and the universality, then it is obvious that the individual needs a mediation, and thereby an authority, in order to progress on this path. One has to renew the position of the master – it is not true that one can do without it, even and especially in the perspective of emancipation.

Badiou is not afraid to oppose the necessary role of the Master to our 'democratic' sensitivity: 'This capital function of leaders is not compatible with the predominant 'democratic' ambience, which is why I am engaged in a bitter struggle against this ambience (after all, one has to begin with ideology).'

We should fearlessly follow his suggestion: in order to effectively awaken individuals from their dogmatic 'democratic slumber,' from their blind reliance on institutionalised forms of representative democracy, appeals to direct self-organisation are not enough: a new figure of the Master is needed. Recall the famous lines from Arthur Rimbaud's 'A une raison' ('To a Reason'):

> A tap of your finger on the drum releases all sounds
> and initiates the new harmony. A step of yours is
> the conscription of the new men and their
> marching orders.
> You look away: the new love!
> You look back, — the new love!

There is absolutely nothing inherently 'Fascist' in these lines – the supreme paradox of the political dynamics is that a Master is needed to pull individuals out of the quagmire of their inertia and motivate them towards self-transcending emancipatory struggle for freedom.

What we need today, in this situation, is a Thatcher of the Left: a leader who would repeat Thatcher's gesture in the opposite direction, transforming the entire field of presuppositions shared by today's political elite of all main orientations.

ALEXIS TSIPRAS

18

EUROPE WILL BE EITHER DEMOCRATIC AND SOCIAL OR IT WILL NO LONGER EXIST

From an interview by Srećko Horvat, Athens, May 2013

On July 1st Croatia should become the newest member-state of the EU. Having in mind the Greek experience, how do you see the enlargement of the European Union during its biggest financial and political crisis? What future does Croatia have in the EU?

We are at a phase where Europe is being redesigned. The goal is to have a two-speed Europe, a union of states where the surplus countries will be taking the role of the rider and the deficient countries that of the horse. We're talking about a Europe where monetarism, harsh austerity and the demolition of the society will be the answer, no matter what the question might be. It is easy for someone to predict what is to be expected for Croatia. Inside or outside the euro, the state of Croatian workers will constantly deteriorate, the future of young people will be more and more uncertain and dark, and pensioners' dignity will be hit harder and harder. We must prevent this development. The free-markets system can no longer promise constant prosperity and growth for all. After the 2008 crisis, this system collapsed, and all its hostility spread out into society. We cannot go on much longer like this. Europe will be either democratic and social or it will no longer exist. Therefore we need a historic change of direction. In order to make this happen, the peoples of Europe must take the situation into their own hands through struggle, ruptures and solidarity. It is through all forms of social resistance that a new and alternative way for the whole of Europe will emerge.

There is a famous quote by Henry Kissinger, that 'nothing important can come from the South' and that 'the axis of history starts in Moscow, goes to Bonn, crosses over to Washington, and then goes to Tokyo'. Is this still valid? Or do we live in profoundly changed international environment? In this respect, can something 'important' really come from the South? Do you think the countries of the periphery of EU; Greece, Spain, Portugal, and also including Slovenia and Croatia, can form a new axis of resistance?

I don't know what these abstract historical words mean. Vietnam for example, is not part of this axis, and is neither being referred to in this phrase, but there Kissinger's superpower was determined by farmers wearing thongs. At the time of Kissinger, Latin America was the sum of bloodthirsty, pro-American dictatorships. Today many people are looking in that direction and thinking that 'something important can come from the South'. It is the social resistance movements that rewrite history, otherwise we would have the same system of power for centuries. This is the big challenge for the peoples of Europe: to unite, to stand up against neoliberalism, to put the need for democracy and a life with dignity as a direct political objective. The European South is the first outbreak of change because the countries which constitute the South find themselves in the same situation. But change won't come through a South–North clash. It has to come through one movement, which will unite all European workers, Northern and Southern, against the supremacy of the capital and the markets.

The crisis in Greece is not waning and according to recent statistics, when it comes to unemployment, the collapse of the health-care system and public services, people left without food, etc. the situation is only getting worse. Recent statistics show you could be the new prime-minister. And here we come back to the old Leninist question: 'What is to be done?' Can you explain to us what concrete measures SYRIZA would take if it were to form the government? What to do about reaching agreements with the Troika, how to fight high unemployment, how to resolve the crisis?

The explosion of unemployment and the demolition of the social state are something more than side effects of the crisis. They are the goals of a policy which is has being implemented in Greece, and is gradually being promoted to other 'weak' countries in order to deliver the most perverse neoliberal fantasies. The Left, which brings together more and more social support, will be called on to solve a fundamental problem: that of how to achieve financial stabilisation, while at the same time supporting weak and vulnerable people, who by now constitute a huge social majority. The care of the weaker members of society will rally the rest of society to our side and will gradually increase the demand and reinforce the economy. At the same time, economic stabilisation will allow us to denounce the Memorandum, to stop the policy of uncontrolled recession, and to negotiate the debt from a more powerful position for Greece and for the whole European South. Our goal is a new deal which will link the debt payment with the growth of the economy, because it is only then that the debt can be sustainable. Germany has known this since 1953, when the issue of its own debt was questioned, after the end of WWII.

On the other hand, we bear witness to a growing popularity of the far right extremist party, Golden Dawn. How is SYRIZA dealing with it at this moment and what would you do if you become prime-minister?
The Nazi extreme right is always a useful backup to the system. This is because it is hostile towards critical thinking, it abhors democracy, targets the weak and those who resist the system, and proclaims its belief as 'order' by going against every form of social protest. Fascists have traditionally made dynamic comebacks to the political forefront when the system is being threatened from the Left. Against them there is the powerful wave of the anti-fascist movement, which expresses itself through action with massive public initiatives, by blocking fascist initiatives, exposing the extreme actions of the Right and also in confrontations in the streets, where they obviously need to avoid falling into the fascists' trap of using violence. Our position is clear: at the political level, the answers must be merely political because this is how democracy should work. However at the practical level, the immunity that these fascist groups enjoy will end. There are laws which define and punish hate crimes and these laws will be applied to anyone who violates them.

How to avoid the mistakes of the past? Do you think social-democracy is still an answer?
Social democracy allied itself willingly to the Right after 1989 and enthusiastically joined the neoliberal doctrines. For a long time, it was indeed the favourite of the capital and the markets as social democracy was considered to be able to

promote deregulation policies with less social reaction. Today with this crisis, social democracy is shrinking. In Germany, it cannot threaten Merkel as it has nothing different to say. In France, it has dissolved all expectations. In the South, it is about to disappear. Let's keep in mind the position of the veteran Portuguese political, Mario Soares, who said that the only honest attitude for the socialist forces would be to form a new alliance with the Left, against the powers of the crisis and of neoliberalism. This alliance is already being put into practice at the base of society, bottom up. However, the social democratic governments no longer have either the disposition, nor the possibility, let alone the credibility, which is required to achieve this. Therefore, the social democratic space is left to shrink while new forces, with new alliances with the Left at their core, come to the forefront.

What about the 'welfare-state'. It is now obvious that the traditional form of 'welfare state' has to be modified, but on the other hand, it is also obvious that the privatisation of the health-care system, education and social security is leading to a radical devastation of society. Can the 'welfare state' still survive? Or, can it perhaps be re-casted as a set of citizens' institutions, as a model of development which forms the basis of social reproduction? In other words, is it just a question of how do we pay for it, or is it also a question of how do we conceptualise and operationalise it through institutions? Do you think this kind of question would be on the table if you were in the position to run the country?
The welfare state is neither a gift, nor a waste of money. It is a system financed by workers' and employers' contributions as well as taxation. It is therefore, a form of redistribution of wealth and the redistribution of wealth itself is a sign of social

progress. Obviously the welfare state must be productive, must provide its citizens with decent services, work under transparent terms and not be spendthrift. But when the economy is growing, as happened the last decades, one would expect and demand the improvement rather than the shrinking of social services. Furthermore, in some countries such as Greece, the welfare state's resources were being systematically looted for decades, through a system of political corruption. The privatisation of social services is not good for anyone, except for the businesses which are waiting to plunder the fields of education, of healthcare and social security and are obviously aimed only at those who have to pay. The defence of the welfare state, and the insurance of sustainability through fair, transparent and reciprocal financing is one of the key demands of the forces that defend social cohesion.

Recently, you attended the funeral of Hugo Chavez. Is Latin America a model for Greece, and what are the concrete steps SYRIZA could or would put into practice if it succeeds in forming a government?
Chavez's Venezuela is the shining example of a country that combines economic growth with a reduction in social inequalities. Chavez clashed in a direct way with powerful economic interests, and won almost all the battles, thereby enjoying broad popular support, while remaining committed to democracy. This case study is of course different from that in Greece, since Venezuela has a far greater problem with poverty and the ability to make policy with its own currency. But it remains a model for us, as it does for the Left around the world, for the creation of social economy, political support of the weakest, the adherence to a policy of growth on the basic criteria of the peoples' interests rather than the small

inancial oligarchy's interests. Chavez did put in action the motto 'people before profits' and convinced us that this world can be changed.

Who are the allies of SYRIZA on the European level?
Firstly, there are the powers within the Party of the European Left (EL). The achievements of the EL are valuable because they exceed the division between powerful and weak states within Europe. The clash in Europe is not between countries. It is between the capital and the markets from one side, and the working people from the other side. We also consider as an ally, any political power which makes a reliable and progressive critique of neoliberalism. Last summer though, when SYRIZA came very close to the major reversal, we found out that our allies are society itself, the people, ordinary people everywhere across Europe. Everybody expected and hoped then that the Left in Greece, the country most devastated by neoliberalism, would make the first step towards a big change in power relations across Europe. We will keep on and we will succeed.

In a recent article published in the *New Statesman*, which already provoked many comments and discussions, Slavoj Žižek claims that what we need today 'is a Thatcher of the Left, a leader who would repeat Thatcher's gesture in the opposite direction, transforming the entire field of presuppositions shared by today's political elite of all main orientations'. On the other side, we have Alain Badiou and his insistence on 'distance from the state'. It seems we are back to the old discussion of the 1960s, when Rudi Dutschke proposed the 'long march through the institutions'. How can this deadlock be solved? What position do you share? And,

if we choose Žižek's position, how to achieve a balance with the existing protest movements?

Žižek has always had a direct and thought-provoking message. What I understand is that he is calling to the Left to claim and retrieve the ideological hegemony. Because the one who has the ideological hegemony, can lay the tracks on which to move trains. I do not know if this requires a leader or a dynamic return of social forces, with the 'crowd' in the forefront. Chavez was an irreplaceable leader, but Mubarak was turned away by the crowd. What I know for sure is that in order for the Left to gain the hegemony, it has to bring out the best in itself, both as a revolutionary and as a reformist force. And this means that the Left must be active and effective both inside and outside the institutions.

In this context, how can we avoid the failure not only of the German and French Left, but also the Greens, who became part of the establishment by losing their previous emancipatory potential? And is a coalition between the Left and the Greens still possible? How is SYRIZA dealing with this question?

The problem has always been how to approach power, without letting that power transmute and assimilate you. This is what has happened throughout Europe during the past decades. Power makes you a 'realist', and in the end it leads to concessions and compromises beyond your principles. The German Greens thought that they were influencing the political agenda, when in fact they had been fully assimilated into the system of political and economic power. Today, with the crisis, things are being redefined: firstly because neo-liberalism does not emerge as the vindicated winner of the Cold War, but as a highly aggressive and destructive system. Secondly, and more importantly, because the masses have rapidly emerged from a state of political apathy in which they were immersed for decades. Under these circumstances, the capitulation of their representatives under the system is a no longer an acceptable situation. As for the Greens in Greece, they failed to establish themselves as a political party, and they are already divided into two strands. We are open to work with anyone who has a clear view of the defence of society against the attack of the capital. In a broad social alliance, the forces of radical ecology could play an important role.

Uniting the Left within nation states in larger and ambitious organisations is perhaps the biggest political obstacle for the Left, especially in developed countries. We assume that the rise of SYRIZA, as was the case with most successful left-wing parties in general, was an organic one. However, in each organic development there are decisive moments and decisions. What were those key moments and decisions for you and SYRIZA, especially from the perspective of offering useful insights for the developments of the Left in other countries?

I think that we had an accurate and convincing analysis of the crisis, and correctly predicted the course of the Memorandum. We highlight the class dimension of the Memorandum, but also the clash between a cruel neoliberal policy and democracy. But most importantly, we refused to get locked behind the accuracy of our line, and on the contrary we talked about a broad unity, beyond individual differences, and we meant it. When those dynamic, spontaneous and massive movements of social resistance erupted, we did not confine ourselves by criticising them from the opposite pavement, nor did we explain to the people what to do. We entered them with all our forces, and took part in their proceedings by expressing our views and listening to the views of others. Thus, society recognised SYRIZA as a reliable and consistent political ally. There is still, of course, a long way to go in order to turn that trust into a political relationship, in order to become more efficient, more active. Political action does not stop at one point, nor does it end. SYRIZA has a declared and clear political goal, which is the abolition of the Memorandum. This allows SYRIZA to address itself to the people. When the target is reached, it will be simultaneously replaced with new goals, perhaps more complex and more immediate. The higher the bar rises, the firmer we must build by our social alliances.

Slavoj Žižek
Alexis Tsipras

19
THE ROLE OF THE
EUROPEAN LEFT

*This conversation took place at the
6th Subversive Festival, Zagreb, May 2013.*[62]

Srećko Horvat: Croatia is accessing the European Union
during its worst crisis. Could you, Mr Tsipras, from the Greek
perspective, tell us what can Croatia expect?

Alexis Tsipras: You said earlier that maybe – or probably – I
could be the next prime minister of Greece. I don't know if
that will happen, but I know if that would happen, nothing
would remain the same, either in Greece nor in the
European Union. Of course, not because a Leftist politician
would become prime minister, but because a radical Left
party would have the support of the people to make radical
changes in a country that has been through a very tough
recession all these years. And after five consecutive years of
recession, Greece is in depression and in a humanitarian
crisis. We have already lost 25 per cent of the GDP, we have
30 per cent of official unemployment, and especially among
young people, where unemployment is more than 60 per
cent. And all these programmes were implemented because
of the debt crisis. But I want to say something: when the
Troika came to Greece, the public debt was 110 per cent of
the GDP, and now the public debt is more than 160 per cent

of the GDP. This is the meaning of salvation for Greece. They saved the banks and destroyed the society. And of course, the big question is how are we going to change this situation? Let me first give some points of our analysis: we don't believe that this is an accident, we believe that this is a situation that had a goal, and they chose Greece as a guinea-pig for a hard, tough neoliberal policy which had never before been seen in Europe. Maybe we've seen a similar pro-gramme in Chile, with Pinochet, a barbarian neoliberal programme of austerity. And why did they do that? They did that for two reasons: they wanted and they want to make a paradigm for the other European countries, and second, because they have a target, they have a goal to seize public goods, to privatise everything in Greece and to earn money through this procedure. And what did they say at the beginning? They said that the problem is that Greeks are very lazy and they are responsible for this situation; the people, not the banks; not the bankers who gave the loans to the people while at the same time knowing that it was very difficult to repay these loans. And at the same time, they are saying that the problem is that Greeks are lazy and they try to implement this doctrine of shock, as Naomi Klein would say. So the problem is that after a few months, they had to explain why the same problem is occurring not only in Greece but also in Portugal, Spain, Italy, Ireland ... Is every-one in the European periphery lazy? And of course the 'lazy' people started to react. We had the demonstrations in the squares, the people on the streets, demonstrating and trying to react to these policies, and huge protests in Greece had some particular results. First, Papandreou's government fell, second, the Papademos' government fell, and third, one year ago, there was a real confrontation: it was the first time on the European level that a radical Left party looked likely to take the power in the heart of the eurozone. During the elections we were not only against the conservative party of Samaras but also against the financial system of Europe, and we were not alone, because we had the support of the people. You remember that they even published articles in German newspapers in the Greek language, saying that we are 'demagogues' and that we claim that everything is easy. People know very well that everything is difficult – and at the same time they know that it is difficult to continue in these circumstances. So, the situation in Greece deteriorated progressively, but we have shown that we were right in our analysis. First, the crisis in Greece is not a Greek idiom, it is a structural symptom of capitalism and neoliberalism. We believe that the problem is not lazy Greek people, but that we are living at the dead end of the neoliberal project of Europe; we live at the peak of the global crisis of casino capitalism and Europe now is at a crossroads. This Europe is not the Europe of the people, but the Germanian Europe of speculating markets. They often say that SYRIZA – and me – are the danger for Europe, and I want to say that the danger for Europe is not SYRIZA but Germany and Merkel herself and her hegemony at the European level. The solution is the cooperation of people in all European countries, in the periphery and the centre, because this confrontation is not between peoples and nations, this is a war between the labour forces on the one hand and the capitalist forces on the other hand. So, I believe that very soon we will see a radical spring in Europe which will change the situation. If you asked two years ago if there were a possibility to resist and to change the then regimes of the Arab countries, nobody would answer positively. The same is true for now: nobody believes that the situation can change in Europe. But what we need is a Mediterranean Spring, like the Arab Spring.

Srećko Horvat: Slavoj, you also come from the periphery, from Slovenia. In Slovenia we had some signs of the – we could say – Mediterranean Spring, with a strong Occupy movement, trade unions organising protests, etc. You were one of the first on the Left who publicly supported Tsipras at the last elections in 2012. Why do you support SYRIZA and why do you think it is important for the rest of Europe as well?

Slavoj Žižek: It is a beautiful question and I am pleased to answer exactly this question. Alexis already said that if SYRIZA wins, nothing will be the same in Europe anymore. I take this absolutely literally. In what sense? I don't like Al Gore, the American ex vice-president who was a fake ecologist, but he had a minimum of spirit. Remember how everyone expected him to be the president after Clinton, so in a self-ironic move he liked to describe himself as, 'I am the guy who was once the future American president.' And that's the dilemma that I see here. If SYRIZA wins, in a magical retroactive way all history will be read as pointing towards the victory of SYRIZA – this will be the magic element. Which is why I think the entire European establishment is so afraid of the SYRIZA government. Because if SYRIZA wins and does something, it will be the end of a certain European conservative wisdom. Namely, what? I think the fight that SYRIZA is fighting is the fight for the very soul of Europe, and I am talking here, without any shame, as a eurocentrist. OK, it's nice for politically correct reasons to blame Europe for everything; imperialism, colonialism, slavery, but my God, Europe did give – and let's be proud of that – something wonderful to humanity: the idea of radical egalitarianism, of radical democracy, feminism, etc. This is at the core of European identity, and that is what is at stake today. So as Alexis has already stated, who is the danger? – today's defenders of Europe, Brussels' techno- crats or anti-immigrant nationalists, they are the threat to what is worth fighting for in the European legacy. They are the true threat to Europe. Imagine a Europe, and this is now one of the possibilities, where you have economic neo- liberalism combined with elements of anti-immigrant populism; imagine this type of Europe – it is not Europe anymore. So we shouldn't say SYRIZA stands for those who are marginal and excluded. No, SYRIZA stands for Europe! SYRIZA stands for what we should be proud of as Europeans! Secondly, don't buy this rhetoric of SYRIZA as a dangerous experiment. SYRIZA is – to put it very simply – the voice of true reason, moderation and realism. The true dangerous experimentations are being made by those in power; this is the lesson of this financial crisis. And even when Western critics try to portray SYRIZA as playing on this anti-European sentiment, my God, I remember the last electoral congress of New Democracy; I was shocked – all the things that were attributed to SYRIZA by the enemy, were the things they themselves were doing. I remember a lady saying, 'Who are the Germans to teach us, we already had Aeschylus and Sophocles when Germans were still playing football with human heads?' Here you see the hypocrisy of Europe at its purest: the EU gave full support to New Democracy and at the same time they talk about Greek corruption as a problem. But, sorry, New Democracy embodies that what we refer to as Greek clientelism. It is as if you fight corruption and then you support the party that embodies this corruption. So, why SYRIZA? You know what makes me sad: if you look at the history of the so- called radical Left, you have one story which can give honourable results but it has its limits; let's call it the Lula-

Mandela story. A movement with some radical potential takes power and basically accepts the game of international capital. I am not blaming them. First, some limited results can be produced in this way; Lula did do some good things, and one should also frankly ask the people who accuse Mandela and the African National Congress of not introducing socialism – well, wouldn't this have led to an economic catastrophe because of the probable reaction of the international markets? So on the one hand, we have this, let's call it 'the Tony Blair game': we basically accept the neoliberal game and we just want do a little bit more for healthcare etc., or as Peter Mandelson, Tony Blair's 'dark prince' says, 'In economics we are all Thatcherists, the difference is just in our social policies.' On the other hand, I am tempted to name the worst case; we have the radical Left which takes power, or they even prefer sometimes not to take power so when everything goes wrong they can write books and explain in detail why things had to go wrong. There is in theory some deeply rooted masochism in the radical Left. The best books of the radical Left are usually very convincing stories of failures. From Trotsky and his books on what went wrong with Stalin. The uniqueness of SYRIZA is that it rejects this false choice. On the one hand, it is a real, principled, radical Left. On the other hand, they have this courage to take power, and as Alexis said, everyone is aware the situation is difficult. Imagine a SYRIZA victory, because Greece has a clientelist big state which would be threatened by SYRIZA. But at the same time there is hope, and you know why? A couple of months ago when I was in London, I read the Financial Times, and their neoliberal commentator after Tsipras' visit said in very naive and sincere comment, 'But wait a minute, people are presenting Tsipras as a leftist madman, but he seems to be one of the few people who talks reasonably in Europe.' So here we come to the central point, which was also developed by the Greek economist Yanis Varoufakis: something very dangerous is happening in Europe. To put it in old-fashioned words, I think the European political elite is progressively losing its possibility to rule. In other countries, with all his compromises, Obama is ruling, but Europe is losing its compass. We leftists had this ridiculous dream back in the 1950s; that somewhere between Washington and Wall Street the true rulers meet, the top capitalists, the secret committee, and they decide everything. In the case of Europe today, I would even pray for there at least to be this type of secret committee of people who know what they are doing. There is not. Which is why I think the task ahead of SYRIZA is not some crazy, radical measures, but to simply, in a very pragmatic way (which will have very radical consequences) to bring back rationality, to give people hope, to stabilise the situation and so on. Because people are saying, especially with regard to ecology, that we just think about profit, that we are too utilitarian and unethical, and that we should have a more moral attitude. But wait a minute, today's capitalism is not utilitarian, from a utilitarian point of view; today's European capitalism is a nightmare utopia which is leading us all to ruins. I more and more suspect that all this politics of austerity is not really a rational politics, yet it uses some mythical narratives – like the idea of austerity being 'You can only spend what you can produce', etc. which is all my old grandmothers' wisdom. In reality, an economy it does not work like that. Or that idea that if you get into debt that you will have to pay it back. The whole history of the United States in the last 40 years is proof that you can carry on quite well for decades without paying your debts. So what I am saying is that we should become more attentive to the irrationality – which is deeply embedded in our daily reactions – of the present global system. I don't buy everything what Paul Krugman is saying, but once he gave an ingenious answer, when he explained what went wrong in the 2008 Crisis. He was asked, 'What do you think would have happened if we knew all these things years before?' His answer was, 'Nothing, everything would be the same.' That's the tragedy of today's capitalism – even if you know it, you are still following your illusions, as if you don't know it. So again, SYRIZA is not a Greek phenomenon, SYRIZA is something that is one of the few signs for the whole of Europe. We can see this clearly if you just compare SYRIZA with other European countries where there were protests. I have full sympathy with the Spanish people, but if you look at the programme of the 'Indignados', these are general phrases: 'We want money to serve people, not people to serve money' – well fuck it, even the Nazis would agree with that! What do I mean? This general humanitarian point is not enough. I am not forgetting that there are progressive moments – protest movements in Paris or London, but SYRIZA is the only one which brought this negative mobilisation ('I've had enough of it'; 'This can't go on like this') a step further towards an organised political movement. Which is why I think SYRIZA is one of the few bright lighthouses in Europe today. And the test for the people, when you ask them what they think about Europe, is to simply ask them what they think about SYRIZA. If they don't support SYRIZA, then in my vision of the democratic future all these people would get a first-class, one-way ticket to the Gulag!

Srećko Horvat: You mentioned several points which I think could be interesting for the development of our further discussion. On the one hand, you mentioned the European leaders who are completely lost – besides austerity measures they don't have any other model that they could implement in order to achieve full employment, de-industrialisation, etc. On the other hand, you mentioned Lula. Alexis Tsipras was recently at the funeral of Chavez. Further still, in one of your interviews you mentioned that Argentina, after the collapse in 2001, could be a model for Greece? So, my question is the old Leninist question: not only what is to be done, but what are the concrete measures and steps SYRIZA would take if you were to form the government? In some of the interviews, and maybe you could explain this more because the debt question is also pertinent for Croatia, you mentioned that Germany's debt cancellation after the Second World War could be a model followed by Greece. This is one example, but there are other measures as well. So my question actually is, what can the institutionalised Left, namely SYRIZA, do if it gets to power?

Alexis Tsipras: First of all, I think that the situation in Greece is like Germany, but not after the Second World War but after the First World War. There was the Weimar contract, not the Memorandum, but it was also the tough fiscal programme and adjustments that created the Nazis. And this is the big danger for Greece. Of course, the situation in Greece has two sides. The first side is the side of hope that SYRIZA gave, but the second side is the side of terror that the Golden Dawn gave. They already have 10 per cent. We have to understand that these austerity programmes create this terror of neo-Nazism, and we have to stop this development, and we have to learn a lot about the not-so-distant history of Europe. What happened in Europe with the crisis of 1929 and what happened on the other side of the Atlantic; they had the New Deal, and in Central Europe we had the recession – and that is the difference. So you asked what we are going to do, and mentioned that there are a lot of similarities with Argentina after the default. But there are, of course, many differences as well. First, we don't have a national currency connected with another currency. Argentina had pesos pegged to the dollar; we don't have drachmas connected with the euro, we have euros – only euros. And the difficulty for a Left radical government, is that if it comes to an end of the euro, there will be a difficult situation because everybody who has euros would have a chance to buy everything because our national currency would be devalued. So that's one difference to Argentina. The other is that we don't have the productive possibilities that Argentina had. Of course, we have some aspects of the economy that we could reinforce. I think that our nuclear weapon is that we are members of the eurozone. Our disadvantage that we don't have our national currency is at the same time our advantage because we are members of the eurozone, of the euro, and we believe that the euro is like a chain connecting 17 countries. If one link would be broken, the chain would fall apart. This would be a nuclear weapon if the government would have the guts, if the government would negotiate at the European level to get the best for its people. In Greece, we never had a government that tried to negotiate these programmes, but we had governments that tried only to implement the orders because they believed what Thatcher said – 'There is no alternative'. So if there is no alternative, the only way you had to take was the way of demolition, of recession, the way of losing dignity and the sovereignty of the people: this is the disaster in Greece now. So you asked what the first steps a Left radical government would be? First of all, as I said before, everything would change, because politics is a balance of power. So if a radical government were to come to power in the heart of the eurozone, in this or another country, nothing would be the same. If we won the elections in June 2012, we would implement our promises – reject the Memorandum, and reinforce the active demand. We would try to redistribute the welfare and try to tax all the people who don't pay their taxes: big ship owners, etc., because Greece is a special case. You know that during the last decade of growth we were 4 per cent of the GDP lower in public income than the average in the eurozone. And why? Not because the workers and the middle classes didn't pay their taxes, but because the rich didn't pay taxes. Our plan would be a plan of stabilisation by trying to get the money from the rich and give it to the poor. I believe that is very difficult because we are living in a globalised community and we are part of the European Union, so nothing will easily change if we won't have radical changes at the European level. So that's why I said it would be a very hard confrontation between the Left government and our partners. That's why I believe that we need alliances. Our best allies are the people of Europe, not only the people of the south, but at the same time the people of the north. It would be very different if Merkel decided not to implement austerity programmes in the south, the periphery, but to raise the wages of workers in Germany, in the north. Namely, the deficits of the South are at the same time the surpluses of the North. I believe that it is possible to change the situation in Europe if the balances change and if we try to implement a solution along the lines of the proposals that many progressive economists, such as Varoufakis or Stuart Holland, have already suggested. And if we try to convince our partners, with support from the people and especially from the South and peripheral countries, for a European Summit on the subject of public debt similar to the one that happened in 1953 in London. How did the economical miracle of Germany after the Second World War happen? Well, there was an international summit in London which decided upon the cancellation of a very big part of the German debt, around 60 per cent, a moratorium for the repayment, and a growth deal – if Germany had growth, they would pay; if they didn't, they wouldn't pay. And that's why Germany now is the main hegemonic force in the whole of Europe. So, we believe that this is the European solution, the win-win European solution. Otherwise, there is no chance for Europe.

Srećko Horvat: So, first let's ask who could be the potential allies in this struggle? And secondly, we know that Alexis is a big fan of football, so to use this language, what will happen if the ball really ends up in our hands? If we have in front of our eyes the experience of the German Left and the German Greens, after '68, when they got into the institutions, are we not returning to the old Rudi Dutschke dilemma about 'the long march through the institutions'. So, my question is, if SYRIZA gets the ball into their hands, how can we avoid the mistakes of the past?

Slavoj Žižek: Very briefly, an answer to the second question. You know, there is a big difference in the very basic situation. After '68, for the Green party in Germany and Social-Democrats, capitalism and the welfare state were still not in a crisis, there was still a big field of opportunities, while today the systemic crisis is very present and this is why the return to the old welfare state is not a solution. And here I also agree with Alexis' subtle hint that with all our sympathies with Latin America, I don't believe in this simplistic story of the European Left: 'Look, Europe is in a crisis, Latin America is doing well, so we should simply follow the Latin American way.' It is not as simple as that. What I want to emphasise, as you correctly pointed out, is this question of alliances. This is my old motto, but I would like to repeat it. I am not fascinated by the big revolutions; you know, one million people on Tahrir Square, a kind of collective orgasm, we all cry with them and we are united. Yes, that's good, but for me the real question is – the morning after. I can imagine the triumph, and all Athens crying if you win, but then? What interests me, and you as well because you are a serious guy, what will your victory mean in the lives of ordinary people when life returns back to normal? And here what you pointed out: the idea that it's a question of intelligent alliances; this comment could be misinterpreted – do you just want to take from the rich and give it back to the poor? For we all know it is not only this simple redistribution, one has to be very careful here. Since we will, for at least some decades, still live in capitalism, I will posit the somewhat mysterious concept of 'patriotic bourgeois', as we called it in the old communist days. This refers to capitalists, who, because of their situation are not just part of some international exploitative mafia but have genuine interest in producing for the people, etc. So I think that it is crucial that in these redistributive gestures that you outlined, that it is not just generally a strike at the rich, but that it should be a very carefully planned strategy. Crazy as it will sound, but I dream that SYRIZA should – within the global redistribution – make life easier even for truly productive capitalists. The problem of Greece is a very specific one; it's again the link of state clientelism with international banks which as every intelligent economist will tell you, is even bad for the truly local productive class. That would be for me, and maybe I am crazy here, a true triumph for SYRIZA – not only will it be better for workers, but if you are a good honest capitalist, you should vote for us! And I am ready to come to you and be some voice for capitalism in SYRIZA. Secondly, your words about Golden Dawn are also important. It is not a Greek peculiarity. It's not, 'stupid Greeks, you didn't find your way so you are escaping to fascism.' I see the Golden Dawn as just one aspect of an unfortunate trend all around Europe, of how here in Croatia, and also in Slovenia, public discourse is changing. Here the Catholic Church openly celebrates the anniversary of Ante Pavelić, etc. And even generally, I noticed how in the last decades there is a subtle rewriting of the Second World War, with many conservative historians, like Niall Ferguson, emphasising that it wasn't as simple as the good side winning, but that it was much more ambiguous. And what goes with this is exactly the rehabilitation of soft fascism. They say, OK, Hitler was bad, but maybe Mussolini, Franco, etc. were not such bad guys, etc. It is a general tendency, and this is what worries me, that things which were unthinkable in Europe thirty years ago, when there was a pact that Europe was founded on antifascism, and when one didn't talk to the successors of fascist parties, that this is now all changing. And thirdly, we have the banks. On the one hand, one should not fetishise banks. Today's dynamic economy needs banks, the pseudo-Keynesian idea of 'Not Wall Street, but Main Street' is too simple – banks as such are not a problem. But, if we go into debt – what austerity measures theories are trying to sell us is, 'You work hard, I borrow, now I don't want to pay you back', but if you look really closely at how things function in indebted countries, it is never a situation like this – 70 or 80 per cent of the money is speculative, virtual money, with no coverage in real commodities, etc. Or take the example of Iceland, where a couple of private speculators succeeded in ruining the entire state. And I think sooner or later we will have to confront the problem that simply, even in the interest of capitalist production, the ongoing banking system cannot perform its function. I don't have a precise answer, but some kind of popular state regulation of banks will have to be enacted. If banks are allowed to function the way they function now, it will be an obstacle in the long term even for successful capitalist reproduction. So we will here, as you said, really need broad unorthodox alliances where it is crucial to convince people that SYRIZA shouldn't simply initiate a crazy leftist revolution; SYRIZA should even modernise the Greek state, make it finally efficient and even a much more 'bourgeois' state. And this is a chance for SYRIZA – you will have to do the decent job that the capitalist ruling class wasn't able to do for themselves. But as you said, you will need a lot of wisdom. Because this orthodox leftist temptation – 'let's not betray our principles, let's be radical' – did you notice how in the last decade the radical Left, and that's why I admire you, secretly they didn't even want to have power, they prefer to be these negative prophets. You have a unique chance; I am an atheist, but I will say it as an atheist – all our prayers will be with you.

Srećko Horvat: I would like to return to a previous point made by Slavoj – to the day after. SYRIZA is known as a very broad coalition, and you actually succeeded in getting rid of the classical problem of all leftist groups – and that's fractionism. And there is a great article written by Georg Lukács called 'Hotel Abgrund', in which you have this hotel where all the leftists are either drinking wine or having fights among themselves, but the abyss is somewhere near. I think SYRIZA actually perceived this abyss, and that you succeeded in getting rid of the fractions. The first question is, how did you do this thorough job and build this broad coalition, because when I was in Athens two or three weeks ago you actually said that SYRIZA is now turning into one party and not a coalition anymore?

Alexis Tsipras: If I want to be honest, I have to say that even we didn't understand how that happened. I believe that people made this change in SYRIZA, not SYRIZA itself. One year ago, before the first elections of May 2012, we discussed how we were going to the elections, and I had the feeling that something would change, and of course it was a crazy dream that we were near to power, but we proposed to our comrades to change the typical registration papers you give before elections, and to be not a coalition but a party, because the electoral law wouldn't give a coalition the bonus of 50 members of parliament if we would be the first party; that's the crazy law in Greece, and that's why we have only 71 members in parliament even if we only had 2 per cent difference compared to the first party. So I proposed to change the official papers and try to get the bonus if we would be the first in the elections. And everybody believed that I was crazy, because nobody, even me, believed that there was a possibility to be so close to taking power. If I made the proposal for unification, to transform the coalition into a unified party before the first election, nobody would have accepted this proposal. But on the same day, the day of elections, the voters, the people gave us the order to make this transformation, to be the leading force, to try to unite all the Leftist forces, and not only the

Leftist forces. If you see the election results, you will see a great division: class division and age division. The people who voted for us were younger people, and workers and the middle class. In the labour-rich parts of Greece we had 40 per cent, in the bourgeois regions we had 15 per cent, and when it comes to people aged between 18 and 45, we had 45 per cent. And when it comes to those aged over 60, we had 15 per cent, so it was a joke during the elections – if we want SYRIZA to win we have to lock our grandmothers and grandfathers in our rooms! I have to say that this is a very big transformation in people's belief system, and I believe that what happened with SYRIZA is not an incline of the majority of people to the radical Left, but a radical change of the people who try to think outside of political taboos; they wanted a big and radical change and they trusted us as the only political power in Greece who would do what we promised. And we also still have our hands clean. Nobody expects SYRIZA to change the situation suddenly, but everyone expects us not to change our positions, even if we are attacked from our enemies.

To hear the Q&A session which followed this discussion, please go to http://www.youtube.com/watch?v=aUh96oXYt18

NOTES

1. Quoted from http://www.spectator.co.uk/the-week/leading-article/8789981/glad-tidings/.
2. Quoted from http://www.rationaloptimist.com/. See Matt Ridley, *The Rational Optimist: How Prosperity Evolves, New York*: Harper 2011.
3. Steven Pinker's *The Better Angels of Our Nature: Why Violence Has Declined*, London: Penguin Books 2012.
4. Karl Marx, *Capital*, Volume I, New York: International Publishers 1967, p. 254–255.
5. Op.cit., p. 236–7.
6. 'Thank you, Germany, my soul is burning! Thank you Germany, for the lovely gift. Thank you Germany, many thanks, Now we are alone no longer, And hope returns to our destroyed homeland'
7. J. Le Goff, *Your Money or Your Life*, Zone Books, New York, 2011, p. 39.
8. For an elaboration on this thesis, see Maurizio Lazzarato, *The Making of the Indebted Man*, Semiotext(e), 2012.
9. Franco Berardi Bifo, *The Uprising: On Poetry and Finance*, p. 84.
10. See Yoji Koyama, 'Impact of the Global Financial Crisis on the

Western Balkan Countries: Focusing on Croatia', a conference paper presented at 'Global Shock Wave: Rethinking Asia's Future in Light of the Worldwide Financial Crisis and Depression 2008-2010', Kyoto University, Kyoto, September 25–26, 2010.

11. Slavoj Žižek, 'Ethnic Dance Macabre', *Guardian* Manchester, Aug 28, 1992.

12. 'EU Spend a Whopping €20M To Ease Fears About Croats', Dec 25, 2012, http://www.croatiaweek.com/eu-spend-a-whopping-e20m-to-ease-fears-about-croats/.

13. For a detailed overview of the situation in Croatia, the period of 'transition' and new protest movements, see: Igor Štiks & Srećko Horvat, 'Welcome to the Desert of Transition. Post-socialism, the European Union and a New Left in the Balkans', Monthly Review, 2012, Volume 63, Issue 10 (March): http://monthlyreview.org/2012/03/01/welcome-to-the-desert-of-transition and Toni Prug, 'Croatia protests show failure of political promise', *Guardian*, 2 April 2011: http://www.guardian.co.uk/commentisfree/2011/apr/02/croatia-protests-economic-slump

14. Private conversation, Ljubljana, 2011.

15. Mitja Velikonja, *Eurosis – A critique of the new eurocentrism*, Peace Institute, Ljubljana, 2005.

16. See Jaroslaw Makowski, 'Erasmus generation, you're Europe's last hope', 24 October 2012, available at: http://www.presseurop.eu/en/content/article/2933441-erasmus-generation-you-re-europe-s-last-hope

17. For a short overview and the thesis that the fascists didn't suddenly multiply in Greece, but gradually, see: Spyros Marchetos, 'Golden Dawn and the rise of fascism', *Guardian*, 19 June 2012.

18. Joseph Goebbels, 'We Demand', http://www.calvin.edu/academic/cas/gpa/angrif05.htm

19. For a detailed overview of how the newspaper was used by Goebbels as a significant instrument for building support for Nazi ideas, see: Russel Lemmons, *Goebbels and Der Angriff*, University Press of Kentucky, 1994.

20. For more info see: Azriel Bermant, 'A dangerous and irresponsible alliance', *The Jerusalem Post*, 8 December 2011.

21. The complete version of Anders Breivik's Manifesto is available here: http://info.publicintelligence.net/AndersBehringBreivikMani festo.pdf

22. Quoted from http://www.presseurop.eu/en/content/news-brief/2437991-orban-considers-alternative-democracy.

23. Gary Wills, 'Scandal', *The New York Review of Books*, 23 May, p. 6.

24. Another cynical strategy is to blame the enemy: the US Catholic authorities referred to a research project whose alleged result was that the sexual permissiveness of the 1960s on was to be held responsible for the widespread paedophilia prevalent in the Church...

25. For example, while soldiers were standing in line for their meal, a common vulgar joke was to poke one's finger into the ass of the person ahead of you and then to withdraw it quickly, so that when the surprised person turned around, he did not know who among the grinning soldiers behind his back had done it. A predominant form of greeting to a fellow soldier in my unit, instead of a simple 'Hello!', would be 'Suck my dick!' ('Pusi kurac!' in Serbo-Croat); this formula was so standardised that it completely lost any obscene connotation and was pronounced in a totally neutral way, as a pure act of politeness.

26. Robert Pfaller, 'The Potential of Thresholds to Obstruct and to Facilitate. On the Operation of Displacement in Obsessional Neurosis and Perversion' (unpublished paper, 2002).

27. Bernard-Henri Lévy, 'Angelina Jolie, Bosnia in Her Heart', *The Huffington Post*, 2 February 2012, available at: www.huffingtonpost.com/bernardhenri-levy/angelina-jolie-bosnia_b_1290338.html

28. Giorgio Agamben, *Remnants of Auschwitz*, New York: Zone Books 2002, 21.

29. Bernhard Schlink, *The Reader*, New York: Vintage Books 1998, 157.

30. See www.youtube.com/watch?v=ya46wfeWqJk

31. See www.bhraja.ca/Vijesti/BH-teme/%22D%C5%BEelatov-%C5%A1egrt%22-%11-tekst-zbog-kojeg-je-Kusturica-tu%C5%BEio-Nikolaidisa.html

32. See www.e-novine.com/stav/56790-ostalo-velike-Srbije.html

33. See Slavenka Drakulić, 'Can Hollywood tell the truth about the war in Bosnia?', *Guardian*, 17 February 2012, www.guardian.co.uk/commentisfree/2012/feb/17/bosnia-in-the-land-of-blood-and-honey

34. See S. Horvat and I. Štiks, 'Welcome to the Desert of Transition! Post-Socialism, the European Union, and a New Left in the Balkans', *Monthly Review*, March 2012, http://monthlyreview.org/archives/2012/volume-63-issue-10-march

35. I owe this reference to the writer and director of the Stefan Zweig Zentrum – Klemens Renoldner.

36. Stefan Zweig, 'Bei den Sorglosen', in: *Die schlaflose Welt 'The Sleepless World'. Essays 1909-1941*, S. Fischer Verlag, 4. Auflage[4th edition], 2003, p. 110–111.

37. Stefan Zweig, *ibid*, p. 427–428. From the 1943 Viking Press edition of *The World of Yesterday: An Autobiography* by Stefan Zweig, thanks to GoogleBooks, accessed 12.09.2013.

38. Stefan Zweig, Die Zukunft des Schreibens in einer Welt im Krieg ['The Future of Writing in a World at War'] (New York Times Book Review, 28. Juli 1940[28 July 1940]), published in

Zweigheft, 6, Mai 2012, Stefan Zweig Zentrum, Salzburg, p.17.

39. Ibid, str. 9–10.
40. Robert Menasse, *Der Europäische Landbote (The European Rural Courier Messenger)*, Paul Zsolnay Verlag, Wien, 2012, p7.
41. Davor Butorac, 'Nisam rasist, ali nije ugodno...', Jutarnji list, 7. 2. 2013.
42. See O. Mannoni, 'Je sais bien, mais quand meme...' in *Clefs pour l'imaginaire ou l'Autre Scene*, Editions du Seuil, Pariz, 1968., str. 9-33. The English translation can be found here: http://ideiaeideologia.com/wp-content/uploads/2013/05/Mannoni-I-know-very-well.pdf
43. Available here: http://vimeo.com/56909912
44. See Etienne Balibar, *Nous, citoyens d'Europe: Les Frontières, l'Etat, le peuple*, La Découverte, Paris, 2011.
45. See Mauricio Lazzarato's *The Making of the Indebted Man*, Cambridge: MIT Press 2012.
46. Op.cit., p. 139.
47. I rely in this description of Lazzarato's theory on Martin O'Shaughnessy – see http://lafranceetlacrise.org/2012/08/23/lazzarato-and-the-governmental-power-of-debt-la-fabrique-de-lhomme-endette-or-the-making-of-indebted-man.
48. Karl Marx, *Capital*, Vol. 1, London: Penguin Books 1990, p. 280.
49. See Ivan Nagel's outstanding *Autonomy and Mercy*, Cambridge: Harvard University Press 1991.
50. At a more elementary level of the symbolic order, a speaking being is *a priori* indebted to the Other, 'guilty' in a purely formal sense (elaborated, among others, by Heidegger in his *Sein und Zeit*), and the task of psychoanalysis is not to teach the subject how to fully assume this debt, but to suspend this debt, to see its illusory nature. The paradox is that the obverse of this *a priori* debt is a loss ('symbolic castration')

constitutive of a speaking being: what makes me indebted is not some gift I got from the Other, but *the very loss I suffered as the price to be incorporated into the Other.*

51. Peter Sloterdijk, *Zorn und Zeit*, Frankfurt: Suhrkamp 2006, p. 55.

52. One witnessed the same situation in state-socialist regimes: when, in a mythical scene from Soviet hagiography, Stalin takes a walk in the fields, meets there a driver whose tractor broke down, and helps him to repair it with a wise advice, what this effectively means is that not even a tractor can function normally in a state-socialist economic chaos.

53. See Alexis Tsipras & Slavoj Žižek, 'The Role of the European Left', discussion in Zagreb, May 5, 2013, Subversive Festival: http://www.youtube.com/watch?v=aUh96oXYt18

54. http://greece.greekreporter.com/2013/05/21/zizek-wants-gulags-for-syriza-rivals/

55. Believe it or not, the official name of the group of people working for Nea Democratia is called 'The Truth Team'. See: http://www.truthteam.gr which is actually a copy of Obama's team, having the same name: http://www.barackobama.com/truth-team/

56. http://english.alarabiya.net/en/News/world/2013/05/20/Greek-neo-Nazis-threaten-to-mobilize-against-mosque-.html

57. Borislav Škegro, 'Hrvatsku može spasiti samo netko poput Margaret Thatcher', Jutarnji list, 9. 4. 2013. http://www.jutarnji.hr/hrvatsku-moze-spasiti-netko-poput-margaret-thatcher/1095894/ (The link is worth opening because it contains a photo showing the first Croatian president Franjo Tuđman, together with his leading economist, drinking champagne with the 'Iron Lady')

58. See: http://www.croatiaweek.com/youth-unemployment-hits-record-high-in-croatia-51-6/

59. English version of the interview available here: http://www.ditext.com/heidegger/interview.html

60. See: Etienne Balibar, 'A new Europe can only come from the bottom up', openDemocracy, 6 May 2013, http://www.opendemocracy.net/etienne-balibar/new-europe-can-only-come-from-bottom-up
61. http://www.opendemocracy.net/sandro-mezzadra/as-europe-is-provincialized-reply-to-etienne-balibar
62. The conversation took place in Zagreb on 15.5.2013. at the 6th Subversive Festival. For the whole debate including a Q&A see: http://www.youtube.com/watch?v=aUh96oXYt18

istrosbooks

Istros Books is a boutique publisher of contemporary literature from South East Europe, based in Bloomsbury, London. We aim to showcase the very best of fiction and non-fiction from the Balkan region to a new audience of English speakers: bringing the best of European writing through quality translation.

Amongst our authors we have European prize winners, polemic journalists turned crime writers and social philosophers turned poets. Uninhibited by Creative Writing courses and market forces, all our authors write out of passion and dedication to stories and themes that they believe in, so you can always expect to find fresh and exciting writing at Istros Books.

LOOK OUT FOR OUR
2014 TITLES

Hamam Balkania by Vladislav Bajac – A tale of East and West; of Christianity and Islam and the age-old struggle between them. Based on the true stories of two young recruits to the Sultan's personal guard, this story of sixteenth century Ottoman intrigue is interspersed by modern-day conversations between the author and his friend, Orhan Pamuk

Mission London by Alek Popov – Combining the themes of corruption, confusion and outright incompetence, Popov masterly brings together multiple plot lines in a sumptuous carnival of frenzy and futile vanity, allowing the illusions and delusions of the post-communist society to be reflected in their glorious absurdity!

Death in the Museum of Modern Art, stories by Alma Lazarevska – Considered by many to be the undiscovered genius of contemporary Bosnian literature, this sublime collection brings together six stories, each unique and yet linked by the dreadful omnipresence of the last Balkan war.

The Great War by Aleksandar Gatalica – published in the centenary year of the start of WWI, this book offers a unique insight into some of the personalities from all warring sides; depicting the destinies of winners and losers, generals and opera singers, soldiers and spies.

False Apocalypse by Fatos Lubonja – a fascinating account of the financial and social meltdown which followed the liberation of Albania from decades of oppression, re-told by one of the old regime's most renowned political prisoners.